Please renew or return items by the date
shown on your receipt

**www.hertfordshire.gov.uk/libraries**

Renewals and enquiries: 0300 123 4049

Textphone for hearing or 0300 123 4041
speech impaired users:

L32 11.16

Hertfordshire

INTRODUCTION TO

*Heraldry*

# Introduction to Heraldry

## STEFAN OLIVER

David & Charles

A QUINTET BOOK

First published in the UK by
David & Charles in 2002

ISBN 0 7153 1512 9

Conceived, designed and produced for David & Charles by
Quintet Publishing Limited
6 Blundell Street
London
N7 9BH

Editors: Robert Stewart, Shaun Barrington
Art Director: Peter Bridgewater
Designer: Linda Moore
Illustrator: Stefan Oliver

Typeset in Great Britain by Central Southern Typesetters, Eastbourne
Manufactured in Hong Kong by Regent Publishing Services Limited
Printed in Singapore by Star Standard Pte Ltd
for David & Charles
Brunel House, Newton Abbot, Devon

# Contents

| | |
|---|---|
| Introduction | 6 |
| The Origins of Heraldry | 20 |
| The Heralds | 28 |
| The Colours of Heraldry | 32 |
| Heraldic Accessories | 35 |
| Armorial Bearings | 53 |
| The Animal Kingdom | 59 |
| Plants and Inanimate Objects | 80 |
| Additions to Arms and Marshalling Arms | 96 |
| Ecclesiastical Heraldry | 104 |
| Orders of Chivalry and Entitlement to Arms | 106 |
| Modern Usage | 107 |
| Glossary | 108 |
| Index | 111 |

# *Introduction*

FEW PEOPLE can fail to be impressed by the eye-catching display of Heraldic insignia. The magnificence of their colourful array is seen all around us, on public buildings, in churches, on flags, on documents and advertizing materials, on tee-shirts and vehicles — in fact adorning everyday items of all kinds. They provide a decorative and attractive display and a permanent symbol of ownership and individuality in a unique and ever-lasting way and carry the ancient traditions of chivalry, honour and duty into the nuclear age.

In this age of mass production and computerised conformity we are all subject to the powerful influences of television and advertising. The production of consumer items is in the hands of fewer and fewer, bigger and bigger international corporations. The clothes and cars that we buy, the houses in which we live and the foods that we eat, are becoming more and more the same.

People are becoming increasingly interested in finding ways, no matter how small, to assert their own personalities. Heraldry is able to offer people a symbol that is legally personal to them, one which they can pass on to their descendants, which may be used in a great variety of ways to decorate their property in a dignified fashion and which carries historical links into modern times.

People are beginning to understand that Heraldry is not simply a subject of medieval his-

*À te pro te*

tory, but is as alive and meaningful today as it has ever been. Unhappily, misconceptions about Heraldry — many of them deliberately sustained by people who wish to wrap the subject in mystery — have tended to confuse people and put them off the subject entirely. People fear and deride things that they do not understand. Heraldry, being an ancient subject, has customs and a language which are unfamiliar to us and which tend to confuse and hide its true meaning. It is versed in an ancient, though simple and fairly limited, terminology that tends to mystify those who are unwilling to learn it. People are, however, beginning to accept technical jargons as they become more widely used in industry and technology, so that this barrier is happily being rapidly removed.

There is, unfortunately, a quite unjustified social resistance to Heraldry, fostered by those who do not understand the subject. The origins of Heraldry lay in the desire for personal identification. It is true that in medieval times the people who sought this identification were of a high rank in society and that Heraldry became an honour. It is true, too, that it has remained a mark of honour down to our own day. One of the great strengths of our society, however, is that this honour is not confined to a handful of people born into privilege, but is available to anyone who by his own effort or good fortune has been able to take the steps needed to become a 'top person'. There are those who feel that an honour should not be inherited by succeeding generations. But who, having earned for himself an honour, or a fortune, would not leave it to his children? The proposition that anyone in this position would divest himself of everything and tell his children to start from the beginning, as he did, is preposterous. Let those who complain about the unfairness of inherited wealth or honour set about obtaining for themselves that which they purport to despise. Let also, however, those who have inherited an honour, be it an Heraldic device or an ancient title, remember that they are the living representatives of the one to whom the honour was originally granted and that it is their duty to preserve and foster its worth.

At first sight, a large Achievement of Arms, dazzling though it may be in its brilliant colours and array, presents an incomprehensible mass of fine detail that is bewildering to the uninitiated. And if they look up the Achievement in a book, they may be baffled by what they read and left with more questions than answers. What is it all about? Where did it all come from? Why is it so apparently incomprehensible?

This short book cannot unravel all the detail that has accumulated over many centuries; nor can it provide all the answers; the hope is that it will start readers along the path that will lead to a more scholarly and comprehensive study, once their enthusiasm has been kindled and their curiosity rewarded with a preliminary understanding.

# The Royal Arms of England

### MANY COATS OF ARMS ON ONE SHIELD

It has become the practice to display many different coats of arms on one shield and, once this is understood, much more sense can be made of the apparent confusion. The reasons for this are more fully explained further on in the book, when the whole subject of marshalling arms together is discussed in its different occasions. The main reason for doing this is to demonstrate, in the case of royal arms, sovereignty over different lands and in the case of personal arms, to show that the wearer represents families other than his own, that have become joined to his through marriage and who have no one in the male line to represent them.

### THE ROYAL ARMS OF ENGLAND

The display of royal arms changes with the dynastic fortunes of a sovereign. A judicious marriage with an heiress would bring more territory under his control and this would be demonstrated by displaying his spouse's coat of arms with his own, so that they are inherited by the heir. The arms of the United Kingdom, in their present form, have evolved over the years from the Royal Arms of England in the following way.

The arms being gules (red) two lions passant guardant or (gold) have become accepted as the arms of the Duchy of Normandy and have been assigned to the Norman Kings of England. In 1152 Henry II married Eleanor, daughter of the Duke of Aquitaine and that territory came under English rule. Her arms were gules (red) a lion passant guardant or (gold). It is thought that this lion was added to the coat of arms of Normandy and the coat, gules three lions passant guardant or was produced. This device, which became known simply as 'England' has remained the heraldic emblem of that country ever since, even though the lands of Aquitaine in France, were subsequently lost.

In 1308 Edward II of England married Isabella, the only daughter of the King of France. Though she had three brothers, none of them produced an heir and so her son, Edward III of England claimed the throne of France as rightful heir, and in 1340 placed the gold lilies on a blue field of France in the first and third quarters of his arms to reinforce this claim. The French, however, subscribing to Salic Law, decided that the crown could not descend through a woman and chose instead his second cousin, Philip, Count of Valois to be their king. However, England continued to display this claim until it was finally dropped in 1801.

Henry IV of England followed the practice of Charles V of France and reduced the number of the fleurs de lys to three.

Henry V of England restarted the wars against France and was victorious at the famous battle of Agincourt in 1415. In 1420 he married Katherine,

ARMS OF FRANCE

ARMS OF SCOTLAND

ARMS OF ENGLAND

ARMS OF EDWARD III

ARMS OF JAMES I OF
ENGLAND,
VI OF SCOTLAND

daughter of Charles VI, the French King. In 1422 he was on his way to be crowned King of France, when he fell ill and died.

The arms of England remained unchanged throughout the dynastic and disastrous 'Wars of the Roses' when so many of England's nobles and princes were either killed, executed or died in other ways. The Tudors eventually succeeded the Plantagenets as the sovereigns of England following the battle of Bosworth. When Elizabeth I died childless in 1603, the crown passed to her nearest relative, James Stewart, King of Scotland. He became James VI of Scotland and James I of England. Thus the two kingdoms became joined and the arms were altered accordingly. Even though the last piece of French territory had been lost in Mary I's reign, the claim to the French crown was still maintained and the arms became England and France quartered together in the first and fourth grand quarters, Scotland in the second and Ireland in the third.

James I was succeeded by his son, Charles I. These were, however, troubled times and the Royal prerogative and authority was being challenged by a parliament of the people flexing their muscles. Following a bitter civil war, the King was executed and a commonwealth was established, which lasted for eleven years. During this time the Royal arms were suspended and a display of arms for the Commonwealth was devised displaying on a shield the cross of St George, the saltyre of St Andrew and the harp of Ireland, over all was placed an escutcheon of the arms of Oliver Cromwell (the leader of the Commonwealth).

In 1660 the monarchy was reinstated and Charles II, son of the executed Charles I, was crowned. The Commonwealth came to an end and the Royal Arms were restored. In 1662 he married Katherine, daughter of John IV of Portugal, but died childless and so was succeeded by his brother, James II.

James, by his first wife, Anne Hyde, daughter of the Earl of Clarenden, had two daughters. The elder, Mary, married William III, Prince of Orange; he was the son of James II's sister Mary, who had married William II, Prince of Orange in 1641. James II was an unpopular and unsuccessful King and in 1688 William III of Orange was persuaded to invade England and raise a successful rebellion against his uncle. The King fled and in 1689 William and his wife Mary were proclaimed joint sovereigns. As William was an elected King, he placed his paternal arms of Nassau, azure (blue) billety (scattered with small billets) a lion rampant or (gold) on an escutcheon (small shield) upon the arms of England. As his wife was also Queen in her own right they displayed her arms (those of her father) with his, side by side on the same shield.

William outlived his Queen and when he died childless in 1702 he was succeeded (by Act of Parliament) by his wife's younger sister Anne. James II's son by his second wife, Mary of Modena, being brought up a Catholic by his mother, was debarred from succession by the Protestant English Parliament. The escutcheon of Nassau was removed from the Royal Arms. In 1707 Scotland became united with England and the arms were again altered to show in the first and fourth grand quarter, England impaling Scotland (that is placed together side by side) France second and Ireland third quarter.

Since the Commonwealth, the English Parliament had gained considerably in power and when Queen Anne died in 1714 they sought to succeed her, her nearest Protestant relative, ignoring the many who had a better genealogical claim to the throne, but who were Catholic. The crown was offered to George, the Elector of Hanover, grandson of Elizabeth, sister of Charles I.

George I was crowned King of England in 1714 and so began the reign of the Hanovarian House of Guelph. The Royal Arms were changed by replacing in the fourth grand quarter the impaled arms of Eng-

land and Scotland with the arms of Hanover. These are in three quarters, tierced in pairle reversed (the disposition of the quarters, see on to Division of the Field) first gules (red) two lions passant guardant or (gold) – Brunswick; second or (gold) semé (scattered over with) hearts gules (red) a lion rampant azure (blue) – Luneburg; third gules (red) a horse courant (galloping) argent (white) – Westphalia; over all, an escutcheon gules charged with the crown of Charlemagne or (gold) – the badge of Arch Treasurer of the Holy Roman Empire.

In the reign of George III, in 1801, with the union with Ireland, the arms were again remarshalled and became first and fourth England; second Scotland; third Ireland. The pretention to the Kingdom of France was finally dropped. Over all was placed an escutcheon of Hanover with a representation of the Elector's cap placed above it. In 1816 this was changed to a Royal crown, when Hanover became a Kingdom.

In 1837 Victoria became Queen of England but because of Salic laws, she could not become Queen of Hanover. This office passed to her uncle, Ernest. The escutcheon of Hanover was removed from the British Royal arms and they took the form that is still in use today.

*The tomb of the Countess of Hertford in Westminster Abbey.*

OPPOSITE *The magnificent display of the banners of the present Knights of the Bath, in the Henry VII chapel of Westminster Abbey.*

# The Achievements of Arms of Philip II of Spain and Mary I of England

**A**nother good example of several different coats of arms being displayed together on the same shield is that created by the marriage of Philip II of Spain to Mary I Queen of England. It shows the sovereignty (or claim to sovereignty) of a large part of Europe assembled into the hands of one person, by fortuitous dynastic marriages. Philip was a Hapsburg and called himself King of Spain, King of Sicily, Duke of Burgundy, Archduke of Austria and Count of Hapsburg, Flanders and the Tyrol.

His forebears were the Archdukes of Austria and had acquired the rich dukedoms of Burgundy, Brabant and Flanders by marriage.

In 1347 Louis II Count of Flanders married Margaret heiress of John II, Duke of Brabant. In 1356 their daughter married Philip I, Duke of Burgundy. He died in 1361 without an heir and the vacant Dukedom was given by King John II of France to his son Philip, who became known as Philip the Bold of Burgundy. In 1369 he married the widow Margaret, former wife of the previous Duke. His great grandson, Charles the Bold, was killed in 1477 leaving only a daughter, Margaret, as the most eligible heiress in Europe . That same year she married Maximillian, Archduke of Austria and Holy Roman Emperor . Their son, Philip, Archduke of Austria and Duke of Burgundy married Joanna the Mad, daughter of Ferdinand, King of Aragon and Isabella, Queen of Castille.  Spain had been five separate kingdoms that had become united over the passage of time.

In 1198 Alphonso IX King of Leon had married Berengaria, heiress of Alphonso VIII of Castille  and their son Ferdinand III became King of both kingdoms in 1230 when his father died.

In 1282 Peter III, King of Aragon married Constance daughter of Manfred, King of Sicily. They produced two sons, James the elder inherited the senior Kingdom of Aragon, and Frederick, the younger, the junior Kingdom of Sicily. Frederick displayed both his father's arms and those of his mother on his shield quartered, in saltyre (that is he divided the shield into four sections, diagonally and placed his paternal arms in the top and bottom sections and his mother's in the two side sections). Divisions of a shield such as this are called quarterings be there two or two hundred.

In 1409, Frederick's line having ended, the Crown of Sicily was offered to Martin I, King of Aragon which he accepted to become Martin II of Sicily, unusually succeeding his son Martin I. Thus the two kingdoms became united and Martin displayed the arms Aragon and Sicily impaled, that is put together on one shield, side by side.

In 1420 John, King of Aragon married Blanche, Queen of Navarra and displayed a quartered coat of the arms of Aragon and Navarra to signify the union.

In 1479 Ferdinand, King of Aragon (Navarra and Sicily) married Isabella Queen of Castille and Leon. They displayed arms of Castille and Leon quartered in the first and fourth grand quarters (a quarter that is itself quartered is called a grand quarter) with Aragon and Sicily impaled in the second and third

quarters. In 1494 the Kingdom of Granada was recaptured from the Moors and the pomegranate emblem of this Kingdom was added to the display of arms as a quartering in point, pointed.

Their daughter, Joanna the Mad, therefore inherited the whole of Spain, and in 1494 she married Philip Duke of Burgundy.

In 1504 Queen Isabella died and Philip became Philip I King of Spain and Sicily. His son, Charles, was in time also appointed Holy Roman Emperor.

However, when Charles died this title passed to his brother, Ferdinand, who had married Anne heiress of Bohemia and Hungary. Charles' son was Philip II, King of Spain, King of Sicily, Archduke of Austria, Duke of Burgundy and Count of Hapsburg, Flanders and Tyrol. In 1554, he married Mary I, Queen of England. He had hoped to tuck the gold lions of England and the fleur de lys of France that Mary displayed on her arms as further quarterings in his own Achievement (a display of arms of any kind is called an Achievement) but this was frustrated by the obstinacy of the British people. They were worried that their Queen should marry an erstwhile enemy and a Catholic to boot. Mary, who was the daughter of Catherine of Aragon, had been brought up a Catholic and when she became Queen she attempted to bring the country back to the true faith. Unfortunately she tried to use the same bloody methods that her brother had used in surpressing it. It was obvious that she should turn to Philip to help her. He was later to lead an expedition against her Protestant sister, Elizabeth and he was her cousin. Her mother, Catherine of Aragon has been the sister of Joanna the Mad, Philip's grandmother. However, the English people were very much against Philip calling himself King of England, and resistance was so great that he could only declare a dual monarchy. Mary and Philip were each sovereign of their own land and Philip could only place the English arms beside his own, in impalement. The marriage was not a success and he eventually returned to Spain, abandoning both his wife and any idea of acquiring England.

Mary died in 1558 and in 1560 Philip married Elizabeth, daughter of Henry II, King of France. He was disappointed too, in that he was never elected Holy Roman Emperor, though he did acquire the Crown of Portugal in 1580 when John III died, for he had married that King's daughter as his first wife, and he subsequently added the arms of Portugal on an escutcheon to his Achievement.

ACHIEVEMENT FORMED BY THE MARRIAGE OF PHILIP
II OF SPAIN AND MARY I OF ENGLAND

ARMS OF JOHN II,
DUKE OF BRABANT

ARMS OF KING ALPHONSO
IX OF LEON

ARMS OF FERDINAND III KING OF
CASTILLE AND LEON

ARMS OF PETER III KING
OF ARAGON

ARMS OF MANFRED,
KING OF SICILY

ARMS OF FREDERICK,
KING OF SICILY

ARMS OF JOHN, KING OF
ARAGON

ARMS OF GRANADA

ARMS OF JOANNA THE MAD, HEIRESS OF SPAIN

ARMS OF PHILIP I, KING
OF SPAIN AND SICILY

ARMS OF CHARLES I KING OF
SPAIN, ARCHDUKE OF AUSTRIA,
DUKE OF BURGUNDY.

# The Achievement of Arms
## of Viscount Lord Savage
## and his wife Elizabeth

The Achievement of arms of Viscount Savage and his wife Elizabeth, daughter of Lord Thomas D'Arcy (see illustration on page 6) is an example of two many-quartered coats of arms displayed together on a shield, side by side (impaled). In England such an impalement only lasts for the lifetime of the marriage. Any heirs of the marriage do not continue to display the arms of their mother in this way because her paternal arms would be carried into the next generation by her brothers. Arms only become permanently attached to others when they belong to a woman who has no brothers to carry her paternal arms onward and so she, in fact, becomes the heraldic heiress of her father. If there is more than one daughter they become equal heiresses and any quarterings that they have can be added to the paternal achievement by their heirs, to descend permanently through the family.

The first thing to be noticed from the Savage coat is that there is an uneven pattern of quarters, there are more in one half than the other. This should alert you to the fact that this is an impalement. As you look at the shield you will discern that in the top left corner (as you look at it), the first quarter is argent (white) six lionocells (little lions) sable (black). This coat is again repeated in the bottom right hand corner of the middle (as you look at it). Similarly, if you look at the right hand half of the shield (as you look at it), you will see that a coat argent (white) three cinquefoils (five petal flowers) gules (red) are similarly repeated. This confirms that this is an impalement – the arms of two people placed together on the same shield. In this case both paternal arms are repeated. This is only done if there is an empty quarter.

In the case of this achievement the bearers are known. However, if this were not the case, reference books called 'Ordinaries of Arms' might help. There is a correct way of describing the design of a coat of arms and such a description in the right order and using the right terms is called a 'blazon'. Provided that you can arrive at the correct blazon for each of the coats, you could look them up in an Ordinary of Arms. However, though this will tell you to which family each of these coats belongs, only a great deal of patient genealogical research will tell you how they came to be incorporated in this achievement. Fortunately, though there are achievements with more quarterings than this, you are far more likely to come across shields displaying a much less daunting array.

# CHAPTER ONE
# The Origins of Heraldry

ERALDRY has its origins in warfare and stems from the warrior's primitive desire to display an emblem in battle to strengthen his own morale and strike terror into the heart of his enemy. All over the world and all through history examples of this kind of decoration can be found. As soon as man was able to grasp the advantage to be had from using a weapon to hit or pierce his foe, he had also to develop a shield to protect him from retaliation. The large surface thus provided was the ideal vehicle for military decoration. Those early devices were not thought to be hereditary and so they were, really, pre-Heraldic. It is doubtful whether those devices were permanent; and a person may have used different ones on different occasions. It is known, for example, that the Norman knights did not later use the devices with which, if the evidence of the Bayeux tapestry is accurate, they fought at Hastings. By then, however, it was already necessary, because of armour in the form of chain mail and helmets that covered a large part of the face, for leaders and knights to have devices on their shields, flags and standards by which they could be recognized.

The great feudal overlords also found it desirable to have some form of recognizable symbol with which they could authenticate documents and instructions that they issued to their largely illiterate subjects; and so there came into use seals that depicted the overlord on his horse, in battle array, with a shield bearing his devices.

Church establishments also used seals, with a picture of the bishop or abbot, as appropriate, engraved upon them. All the land in Europe was nominally in the hands of kings, who rewarded their followers by giving them land. For the most part kings were wise enough not to give large, single blocks of land to anybody, thus diminishing the risk of powerful territorial magnates setting themselves up as rivals to the throne. Landowners usually held their estates in scattered parcels, and since they were unable to make frequent visits to all of them, the need for seals was greatly increased. Seals, carried by the lords' messengers, were marks of authority, badges of identification.

## KNIGHT FEES

Landowners held their land on the condition that they provide knights to ride to battle when the king required them. This was known as 'knight fee'. Only very wealthy landowners could supply a sufficient number of knights from their own resources and so they, in turn,

would grant some of their land to lesser knights in return for knight fee to ride for the king or for themselves, as required. The more land one acquired, the greater one's power and influence and the more knights one could put at one's own or the king's service.

In the recurrent feudal wars of the time, when knights rode all over the country to fight on one side or another, it was necessary that each of them should wear a badge or symbol of the lord to whom he belonged and on whose side he was fighting. Thus kings and lords adopted some simple object as a badge to distinguish their followers in the field. This practice gained wide acceptance in western Europe, during the Crusades of the 11th, 12th and 13th

*ABOVE RIGHT The tomb of Sir William Clopton, son of Sir Thomas Clopton, displaying (LEFT TO RIGHT) his paternal arms, the arms of his mother Elizabeth Mylde, and his own arms joined on the same shield with his first wife Marjory (daughter of Sir Robert Drury of Suffolk), and his second wife, also Marjory (daughter of Elias Francis of Norfolk).*

*RIGHT Detail of the Bayeux Tapestry depicting the Battle of Hastings between King Harold of England and the invading forces of Duke William of Normandy. The devices that the figures display are not thought to be heraldic because the same figures wear different emblems in different episodes shown in the tapestry, and the descendants of those same individuals did not display the same emblems.*

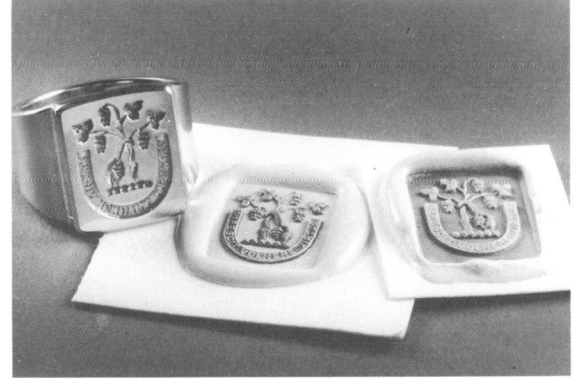

ABOVE *A pruning hook on a crest, on a specially commissioned seal-engraved signet ring; (engraver, Clare Street). The latin motto translates as 'Virtue flourishes by her wound'. Such mottos are not uniquely held: seven families have in fact adopted this example.*

centuries. The Holy Land, the birthplace of Christianity, was overrun by the Muslim Turks, who cut off Christians' access to it. The Pope called on all Christian leaders to take up arms and liberate the Holy Lands. Numerous expeditions were mounted from western Europe, some successful, some not (and some bizarre in the extreme). Men set forth under the sign of the Cross, emblazoned on their cloaks, shields and banners, in different colours and different forms for each country and large group. Their swords were made in the shape of crosses and engraved with pious emblems and inscriptions. Thus the idea of a collective badge to identify a group took universal hold throughout Europe.

## ACCUMULATION OF LAND

Any ambitious lord sought to increase the amount of his land. One of the best ways was to marry a lady who held land in her own right, either because she was a widow or because she was her father's heiress. As the number of young men who died in battle or from disease was high, and the number of wives who died in childbirth considerable, there was ample opportunity by judicious marriages to acquire large estates. A new husband would mark his authority over newly acquired lands by displaying on his seal the armorial bearings of this new land. This practice meant that the mounted figure on the seals was soon dropped in favour of one shield showing all the arms belonging to the different people who had formerly held the land. Some seals also had the main arms engraved on a shield in the middle and the new ones on smaller shields around the outside. The passing of arms from one person to another in this way inevitably led to their being passed from father to son. So Heraldry, as we know it today, was born.

RIGHT *Shown here is the seal of Southwold. The borough has never had a grant of arms.*

## THE IDEALS OF CHIVALRY

In medieval times land was farmed by people who paid a rent in kind, either as part of their crop or in service to their lord, who was thus free to devote himself to other pursuits. Much of his energy was devoted to military activities, either on his own behalf or on that of his over-lord or king. With the example of the Crusades before them, young men prepared themselves by prayer, fasting and ritual to join a company of knights and to lead a life in the military ser-vice of others. So the high ideals of courage, perseverance and generosity to others were bred into them at an early age. In order to ac-quire skill in battle, they spent many hours in practice combat. This led to friendly competi-tions and the idea of the tournament was born. Knights from all over Europe went from one tournament to the next, trying their skill, dis-playing their prowess and winning such prizes and favour as they could. Tournaments were great social events and therefore occasions for brilliant and exaggerated Heraldic display. The contestants hung their shields up outside their lodgings when they arrived so that everyone would know who was in town. People came from miles around to see the spectacle and visit the accompanying fair. On the day of the tour-nament itself, the contestants displayed their armorial bearings on their shields, their Coats of Arms and their horse trappings; they painted them on tents and marquees, on banners and flags, on anything that they could find to make a splendid display. They fashioned on their hel-mets, from wood or softened leather, ornate crests representing animals and birds and all kinds of devices. Their shields were carried around the arena, for all to see, by pages dressed in costumes of exotic and fierce animals. The spectators and their wives wore their ar-morial bearings emblazoned on their cloaks, dresses and surcoats. The whole event was a stunning pageant and carnival. The proceed-ings were presided over by the Heralds, who acted as masters of ceremonies and referees and ensured that things ran smoothly.

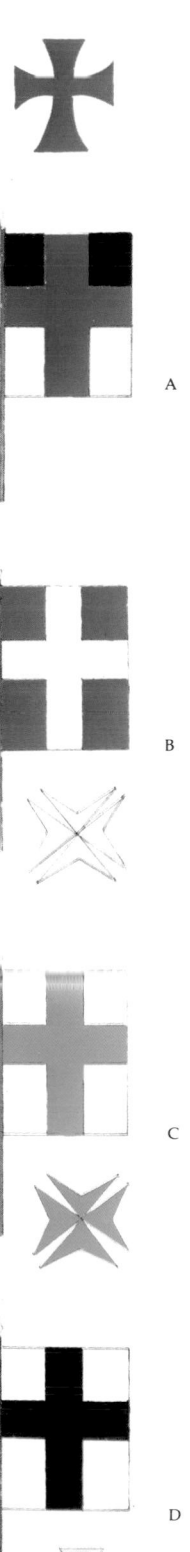

A

B

C

D

The banners and badges of four orders of crusader knights are illustrated here: **A** Templars **B** Hospitalers **C** St Lazarus **D** Teutonic order.

ABOVE *Detail from a military roll compiled in 1448; a jousting tournament.*

RIGHT *Sir William Clopton, son of Sir Thomas Clopton; the ermine spot on the arms he displays on his surcoat distinguishes him from his father.*

FAR RIGHT *Ann Denston, in Long Melford Church, Suffolk; she wears her own arms on her dress and those of her husband on her cloak.*

*The Duke of Normandy, now William the Conqueror,
granting land in England to his supporters, who are
depicted bearing the arms later attributed to them.*

# Display of Heraldry

This is an imaginary illustration and it serves to demonstrate the ways in which Medieval Knights displayed their different devices. Tournaments, as well as providing important training for knights in battle, were also major social occasions and it was very important to put on a good show. They were also occasions when many grudges and grievances were settled and so it was essential that the protagonists conducted themselves in great style.

Lord Stafford is depicted on his war horse with his heraldic device or (gold) a chevron gules (red) emblazoned on his surcoat, his horse's caparisons and on the head shield of his mount. Upon the rein trimming is displayed his badge, the well-known Stafford knot. Atop his helmet is his crest of a swan, with a ducal crown. A page dressed in his livery colours stands holding his lance in readiness. The lance has a pennant, hanging point down when the lance is being used. The page has the badge of his master emblazoned on his chest as does the page holding his master's banner, ready to bear it round the arena before the Lord as he makes his entry. The personal herald, waiting to announce his master, displays the badge on his hat and wears a tabbard of his master's arms. Lord Stafford's pavilion, that serves as a changing room and a store for all his accoutrements, is also made of striped material representing the two main colours of his arms. It is decorated with his knot badge and his standard flies from its centre pole. This long flag whose main purpose is to display his heraldic devices, is made in his livery colours and decorated with his crest and badge. At the hoist it has the cross of St George. Two pages stand ready to display his shield to the crowd. They are dressed as his supporters in the costume of two white swans gorged with a ducal crown.

His wife, Phillipa, daughter of Thomas Beauchamp, who wears a dress of her paternal arms and a mantel of those of her husband hands him a cup. His daughter, Catherine, who was married to Michael de la Pole, Duke of Suffolk, similarly wears her father's arms as her gown and her husband's arms upon her cloak.

If all the knights and their ladies and retainers disported themselves in this way, the great tournaments must have been a riotous display of colour, costume and pageantry as the excitement of the tournament combined with the hurley burley of the accompanying fair, the vendors selling their wares, the jugglers, the tumblers, the fortune tellers and the booths selling spitted pig and other foods. The troubadours and the ale tents; the ringing of the blacksmith's forge as he repaired damaged armour; the games of chance and skill; and the revelry going on far into the night. The event must have drawn people from far and wide and in an era when there was little entertainment, it must have been the highlight of the year.

Through all this festive mêlé the heralds had to hold court. It was their job to make sure that no one appeared in the lists displaying the arms of another. They had to organize and marshall the events, adjudicate on questions of Heraldry and grant arms to those aspirants deemed worthy. The great Lords of the day sometimes granted arms to their followers or retainers that were different versions or allusive to their own as a mark of approval, thanks or favour. The heralds had to record these, check that they were unique and adjudicate in any dispute. A great tournament, when knights were gathered from far and wide, gave them just such an opportunity.

Hugh Lord Stafford Awaiting his Entry into the Lists at a Tournament.

CHAPTER TWO

# The Heralds

ERALDS have been employed by kings and large landowners, principally as messengers and ambassadors, from very early times. They are believed to have come originally from the ranks of roaming troubadours and minstrels, who went from one place to another with their songs and tales. It seems clear that when they were acting as messengers or ambassadors Heralds were free to come and go as they pleased, even across national frontiers. They wore a tabard emblazoned with their master's arms while on 'official duty' and this was supposed to guarantee them protection. An attack on a Herald who was wearing his master's arms was equivalent to an attack on the master. As had been pointed out earlier most lords had land scattered about the country. Heralds were, therefore, constantly travelling and meeting other Heralds and other lords; and in this way they soon began to gather considerable knowledge of the armorial bearings of other people. This gave rise to their second important function, that of staff officer in battle.

## THE HERALD'S ROLE AS STAFF OFFICER

In medieval times many disputes were settled by force. Before embarking upon a dispute over borders with your neighbour, however, it was important to know how many knights he could put in the field against you. Heralds could easily discover this. During a battle itself they were also able to tell their lord, by recognizing the arms, who the opponents were, how many knights they could put into the field and what men they had under their command. They also reported who had left or joined the battle and what forces they had taken away or added. This last function was very important, since many of the combatants were involved only for what they could obtain for themselves; expected allies sometimes held back from the fray and joined it only when it was clear which side was going to win — not always the side with whom they had started out!

Heralds quite often had to decide who had won a battle. At the battle of Agincourt the French and English Heralds watched the day's events together and in the evening reported to King Henry of England that the 'day was his'.

Another important function was the identifying of captives. Important people were held hostage for the ransom that could be gained and ordinary people were put to death. It was obviously necessary to get this right! Heralds also had the unenviable task of identifying the dead. This presented no great difficulty when men

*BELOW Heralds in attendance at the funeral of the wife of Lord Lumley, bearing banners of the Arms of her forebears.*

*FAR RIGHT A roll of arms of the Lord of the Manor of Long Melford Hall in Suffolk, dating from 1044.*

~ 1044 ~ A Roll of Arms of the Lords of the Manor of Long Melford Hall in Suffolk. ~ 1984 ~

fought largely on foot and wore chain mail with open helmets made of iron. The slain could be easily recognized. Knights used to wear over their chain mail a long, loose, padded coat, made of tough material, to help protect them from sword cuts and they adopted the practice of painting their armorial bearings on these. This was called coat armour, or coat of arms, and is the derivation of the phrase, Coat of Arms. If the face of the slain was not recognizable, it was possible to identify him by his Coat of Arms. When, in later years, knights started to wear plate armour and closed helmets, it was impossible to recognize anyone except by his Coat of Arms; the Heralds therefore insisted that knights continue to wear a short surcoat, with their arms painted on them, so that mistakes could be avoided.

When knights charged into battle on their great war horses, wielding huge axes, lances and swords, the force of the impact must have been terrible. Not only was it a question of identifying the dead, but a matter of finding all the right pieces! The use of arms emblazoned on everything, including the crest of the helmet, enabled the Heralds to perform this grisly task. The clash of a couple of hundred knights, charging full pelt at one another and wielding every

*ABOVE A 15th century illustration of the Battle of Agincourt (1415); only the more important figures in the painting are depicted wearing surcoats. The lives of those French nobles thus identified would have been spared after the battle, and ransomed.*

matters and they began to keep lists of all the armorial bearings used at different tournaments, gatherings and battles and of the people who bore them. These lists were collected on long rolls of parchment and were called Rolls of Arms, or simply Rolls. Many of these have survived and they provide a valuable record of early Heraldry. Because the Heralds became so involved in the study and recording of Coats of Arms and in advising and adjudicating on matters relating to them, the business became known as Heraldry. In England the Heralds were incorporated by royal charter in 1484. Since people continued to assume Coats of Arms, without having them registered and recorded at the College, disputes frequently arose over who was the actual owner of a Coat of Arms. Consequently, the Heralds were required to tour the country and record all Coats of Arms, so that they could be registered and disputes be settled. Most of these visitations, as they were called, took place in the 16th century. They form the basis upon which ownership of arms is proved today. The records, however, are not complete, for those were stormy times in England, and in some instances people were unable to answer the call of the visiting Herald, because they were confined to their place of residence. The motive of the Visitation may often have been political and not strictly for the well-being of heraldry. It was a worthwhile exercise for sovereigns to record their supporters and disqualify those who could not support them.

## THE ROLE OF THE HERALDS TODAY

Heralds still have important duties as officers of the Crown, and apart from these duties are very active in Heraldic affairs. Interest in Heraldic matters is steadily increasing and there are now more matters needing their attention than ever before. Their work falls into three categories.

*Confirming arms* There are still people eager to have confirmed to them arms that they have always used, but for which they have to prove a right of descent. The Heralds are glad to help in this work, which involves a lot of patient genealogical research, since, despite the records of centuries, a mass of detail still needs to be recorded.

*Granting arms* Any worthy person may apply for a grant of arms and the Heralds will be pleased to steer the applicant safely through the problems. The steps are roughly these. It is necessary, first of all, to check that an aspirant armiger is not entitled to an existing Coat of Arms. If he is not, it is then necessary to consider with him a possible design and to check that it is not already held by someone. Once this is established and the design is approved by all parties it can be granted to the applicant as the sole right of him and his legal descendants. As well as private individuals, many commercial undertakings and corporate institutions apply

kind of dismembering weapon, must have been sheer bedlam. No wonder so many knight effigies are shown wearing armour! It was probably so battered that it could not be removed.

## HERALDS AND TOURNAMENTS

Because of their knowledge of armorial bearings, Heralds were required to recognize and announce contestants at tournaments and it soon became their responsibility to organize and referee these events. Because of the social nature of the event and the desire by everyone to put on a good display, Heralds were necessary to advise would-be contestants about the choice of armorial bearings that they could use. They were able to make sure that no one chose the arms of another, already in use.

People came to them for advice on Heraldic

for grants of arms.
*Devising arms* The Heralds of Great Britain have jurisdiction only over subjects of the crown. Although many people of British origin who are citizens of other countries wish to register Coats of Arms or varieties of arms belonging to their families to show their ancient lineage, the Heralds cannot grant arms to them. They can, however, following the proper searches, 'devise' arms that could be used and register them in their records so that they will not be issued to others.

The Heralds take great care to ensure that any arms, crests, supporters, mottos, badges or standards are unique to the grantees. This is the point of the exercise. Heraldry exists to identify individuals. There is no such thing as 'Arms of a Name'. The notion that such a thing exists is a deliberate misconception perpetrated by those who would exploit the ignorant for base profit. Knowledge of the outlines of Heraldry protects people from being persuaded to buy a shield of arms with their name on it, on the false understanding that it might be theirs.

## THE LANGUAGE OF HERALDRY

One of the things that puts people off a study of Heraldry is the language. They come up against terms which they simply do not understand. Like many specialist subjects, Heraldry has its own technical language, or jargon, that must be learned. As modern life becomes more and more technical specialist jargons are entering more and more into everyday life; as a result people are showing less resistance to the jargon of Heraldry than they once did. In this way the circumstances of modern life are removing an obstacle to the study of what is, after all, a medieval science.

Heraldry had its origins in western Europe at a time when the predominant language was Norman French and some of that language survives in the Heraldic terms employed today. There are not, however, very many such terms surviving; those that do, chiefly concern the basic matters of design and colour. The simplest way to learn them is to use them; so they will be gradually introduced throughout this book and explained as they appear. One source of endless confusion, however, which must be mastered at the outset, is the question of left and and right.

## LEFT AND RIGHT

Right, called 'dexter', and left, called 'sinister', apply from the point of view of the person carrying, or standing behind, the shield. So 'dexter' means his right as he stands opposite you and you look at him. Similarly, 'sinister' means his left. The dexter, or righthand side of the bearer, is thought to be the most noble, and most Heraldic emblems are drawn facing that way. It is only if they face in another direction that any comment, or explanation, is required.

ABOVE *The Carlisle Roll of 1334 lists Edward III's Commanders.*

LEFT *'Dexter' is the right side of a shield, 'sinister' the left side, from the point of view of the person holding the shield. The upper third portion of the field is called the 'chief'; the mid-point is the 'fesse-point'; and the 'nombril' is the point halfway between the fesse-point and the 'base'.*

CHAPTER THREE

# The Colours of Heraldry

$\mathcal{E}$VEN THE most casual observer may be struck with delight by a bold and colourful heraldic display and it is important from the outset to discuss the Heraldic colours and the ways in which they are used.

The student will soon become aware that the colours of Heraldry are in fact few; it is by skilful combinations of them that bold effects are produced. The colours, or tinctures, as they are properly called, must always be of the clearest and purest tone possible to give a bold, brilliant and unambiguous effect. They were originally chosen so that the wearer would be readily identifiable at a distance, and in the 'pell-mell' of battle, and their bold and striking combination is a vital part of the continuing tradition.

The tinctures fall into three groups: (1) those that represent metals; (2) those that represent colours; and (3) those that represent furs.

## THOSE THAT REPRESENT METAL

The tincture white represents silver and is called 'argent', abbreviated 'ar'. The tincture yellow represents gold and is called 'or'.

It is quite proper to use silver or gold paint, but because of the difficulty of finding suitable pigments that will not blacken with age, it has become the custom to paint these tinctures with yellow and white. In very important documents it is customary to use gold or silver leaf on those parts that should be of these colours.

## THOSE THAT REPRESENT COLOURS

These are listed below, each with its Heraldic term and usual abbreviation. When a Coat of Arms is drawn in black and white, it is necessary to indicate what the tinctures are; a scheme of shading to use for each tincture (which is also shown), has therefore been developed.

There was at one time a custom of describing the colours used by the planets and precious stones and metals. Because examples of this practice may still be found, they are set out in the table below. The colours are red, blue, green, black and purple.

There have been introduced in more recent times the following shades, or stains, as they are called — orange, blood red, mulberry purple and sky blue. Their use is not widespread, although sky blue, as opposed to the true royal blue normally used, is being introduced especially by people connected with aviation and space exploration.

*Many designs, of which a number are shown here, have been devised to represent ermine in Heraldry. Each is a representation of the animal's tail.*

## THOSE THAT REPRESENT FURS

Because of the importance of fur and its common use in contemporary dress, colours and patterns have been devised to represent fur in Heraldry. The use of fur in a variety of forms is common in Heraldry, though it does not necessarily indicate any special rank.

*Ermine* The fur most commonly found is ermine, in its several forms. In northern climates the common stoat, a fierce, small, predatory animal, normally coloured a sandy chestnut, changes its coat to pure white in the winter, but for the tip of the tail, which remains black. Ermine furs were highly prized and, because of their relative rarity and because of the large number of them needed, for example, to line a royal cloak, they were extremely expensive. They were sewn together, still with the tail attached, which hung loose. The Heraldic representation of ermine is white, strewn with a regular black pattern representing the tails. A large number of designs have been recorded in Heraldic representation of these tails.

Various combinations are also used, each with its own name:

| | |
|---|---|
| ERMINE | White with black tails |
| ERMINOIS | Gold with black tails |
| ERMINES | Black with white tails |
| PEAN | Black with gold tails |

*Vair (or Vaire, Vairy, Verre, Verrey, Verry)* The next most common fur is vair, in a variety of forms. It is always drawn as an alternating pattern of rounded or angular pieces of different colours. It is said by contemporary writers to represent the skins of the grey squirrel, sewn belly to back alternately, thus producing the white and blue pattern. Vair is always blue and white, unless other colours are specified, in which case the first colour mentioned is always the piece in the top dexter corner. Vair is met in a variety of forms and these are shown below. A vair pattern of colours other than blue and white is always described as being 'vairy of' whatever the colours specified. The most common forms of vair are vair, counter-vair, potent, counter-potent, vair ancient, and vary.

## DIAPERING

When the Christian knights returned from the Crusades they brought back with them fantastic brocades, woven materials and silks that they discovered in the sophisticated and civilized (compared to their own more robust environment) society that they encountered around the shores of the eastern Mediterranean. Cere-

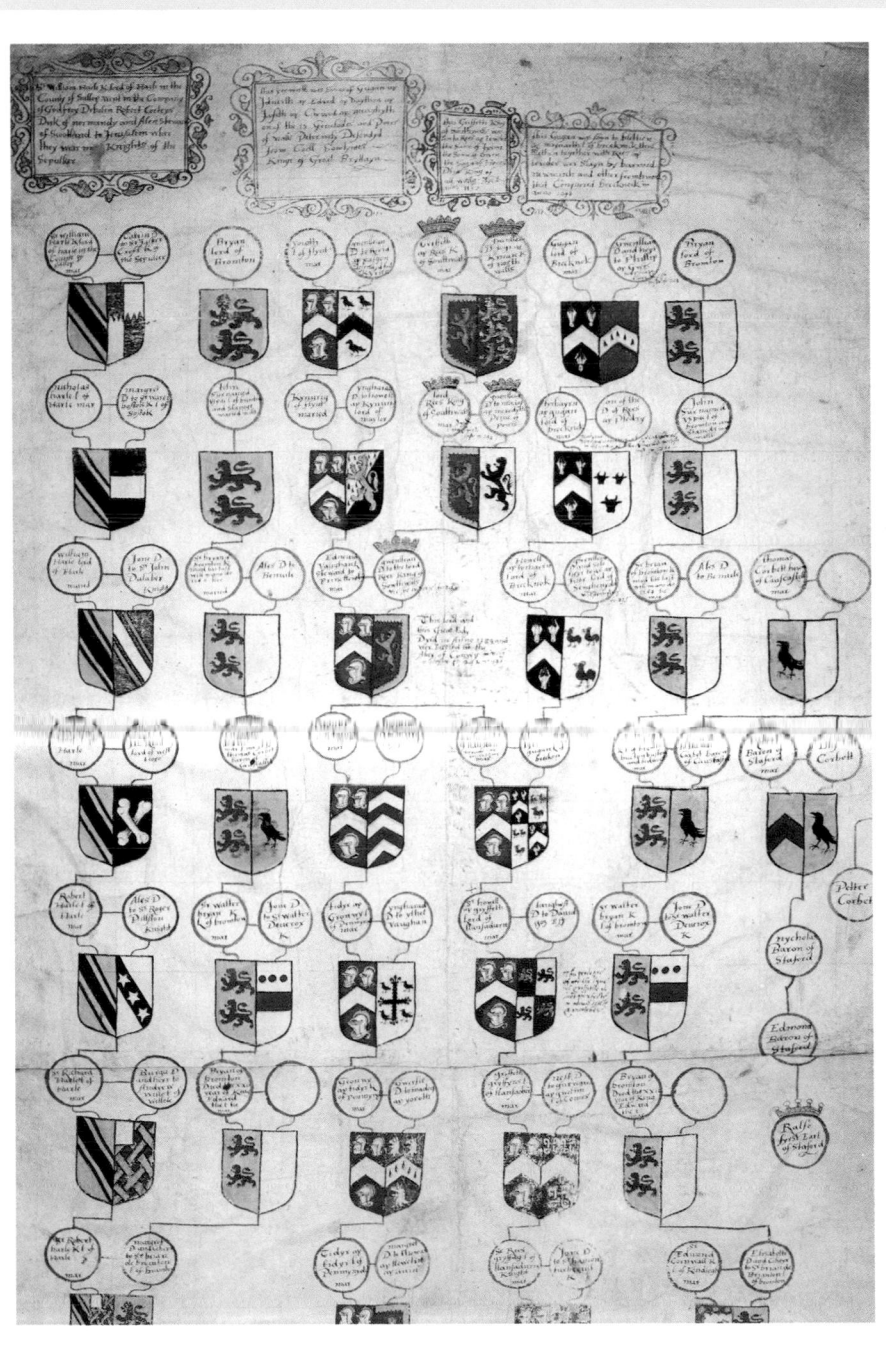

*The 16th century armorial family tree of Anne Hale;*
*note the use of the colours yellow and white in place of*
*gold and silver.*

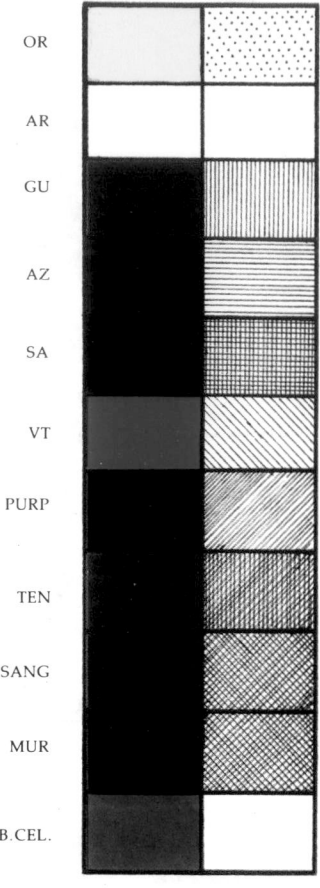

*This chart shows the colours of Heraldry, each with the abbreviation of its name.*

monial Coats of Arms and banners and flags were made of these new exotic materials. Diapering is an attempt to repeat these fantastic patterns, as decorative treatment, on a painted shield, without diminishing the true colour. It was usually carried out in a different shade of the same colour or in painted gold. The patterns usually have an abstract swirl or leaf motif, though there are many examples in which geometric designs or very small, repeated Heraldic devices were used.

## THE RULES CONCERNING THE USE OF COLOUR

There are not many rules, as such, in Heraldry, and by far the most important of them concern the use of colour. For the sake of visual clarity and artistic harmony, these few rules must be observed.

◆ *Never* place a metal on a metal, e.g. a gold lion on a silver shield.

◆ *Never* place a colour on a colour, e.g. a red lion on a blue shield.

◆ *Always* place a metal on a colour or a colour on a metal, e.g. a gold lion on a red, blue, green or black shield, or a red, blue, green or black lion on a silver or gold shield.

◆ A fur can take the place of a metal or a colour.

All good rules exist to be broken. There are plenty of examples of this in Heraldry. They merely strengthen the need for the rules, which developed in the Middle Ages, and still endure today, long after Heraldry's practical use has disappeared. That the rules have survived more or less intact until now must be some kind of proof of their worth.

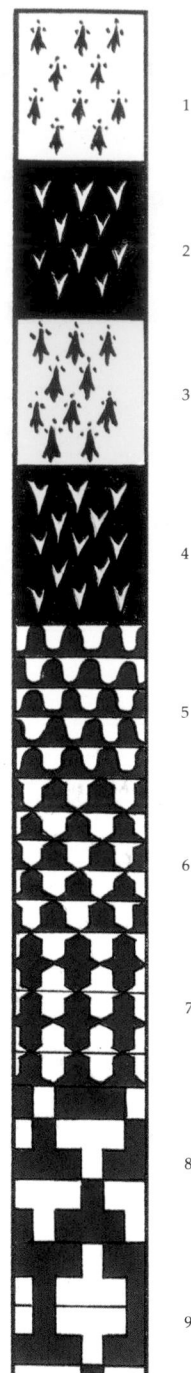

*This chart shows the various combinations representing the tinctures of the two most common furs in Heraldry, ermine and vair.*

*1 Ermine 2 Ermines 3 Erminois 4 Pean 5 Vair Ancient 6 Vair 7 Counter-Vair 8 Potent 9 Counter-Potent*

| THE COLOURS OF HERALDRY | | | | | | |
|---|---|---|---|---|---|---|
| **Colour** | **Heraldic Term** | **Abbreviation** | **Metal** | **Precious Stone** | **Planet** | **Zodiac Sign** |
| Gold | Or | or | Gold | Topaz | Sun | Leo |
| Silver | Argent | ar | Silver | Pearl | Moon | Cancer |
| Red | Gules | gu | Iron | Ruby | Mars | Aries |
| Blue | Azure | az or B | Tin | Sapphire | Jupiter | Taurus |
| Black | Sable | sa | Lead | Diamond | Saturn | Capricorn |
| Green | Vert or Sinople | vt | Copper | Emerald | Venus | Gemini |
| Purple | Purpure | purp | Quicksilver | Amethyst | Mercury | Sagittarius |
| Orange | Tenné | ten | | | | |
| Blood | Sanguine | sang | | | | |
| Mulberry | Murrey | mur | | | | |
| Sky blue | Bleu céleste | B.cel. | | | | |

# CHAPTER FOUR
## *Heraldic Accessories*

IT HAS been shown thus far that Heraldic devices were originally used to identify individuals in the press of battle or to authenticate documents and instructions by way of seals. These devices were painted on the shield, on to the Coat of Arms, onto the horse trappings, on flags, banners and tents and used in every way possible to identify the wearer and owner. With the invention of guns in the 14th century, armour slowly began to fall into disuse, since it was no longer possible for a man both to be mobile and to wear armour sufficiently strong to stop bullet and ball. It therefore ceased to be difficult to identify men on the battlefield and heraldic insignia ceased to be used for this practical purpose by the 17th century. They have continued to be used however, as an artistic and traditional way to identify a person; and shields, though they no longer serve a protective function, have remained the chief vehicle upon which to display armorial insignia.

Armorial insignia are commonly depicted on other accessories and devices besides the shield. The whole assemblage is known as 'the Achievement', which is the correct term to describe the total collection of a person's Heraldic accessories, also called appurtenances. Different countries and customs dictate that Achievements contain different items. This chapter describes the parts of an Achievement.

## THE SHIELD

The shield is the principal vehicle for the display of armorial insignia and is the only essential ingredient in an Achievement of Arms. The devices on the shield are the individual insignia — the armorial bearings — that mark one man from another (See Chap 5). The shield is found in a variety of shapes and these are the outcome of different usages, fashions and times. The principal shapes and styles are shown below.

*The long shield*, which gives the most protection, was used when men fought on foot. It afforded a protection against arrows, as well as in closer combat.

*The short or heater-shaped shield*, which was especially devised for use in tournaments, was strong enough to withstand a hit with a lance. Its shape provided the most protection and deflected the lance from the bearer. It was also called the 'target', or 'targ', after the point at which a knight aimed in a charge at a tournament.

*The square-shaped shield* became more popular when the custom developed of displaying more than one set of armorial bearings on one shield.

*The horsehead shield* is so called because its shape is thought to have developed from the armour plate used to protect the head and face of a knight's horse. It was quite often used by ecclesiastical dignitaries when the military-style shield was felt to be inappropriate.

*The lozenge and oval* Armigerous women customarily display their arms on an oval or a lozenge, since it has always been felt that it is inappropriate for a woman to display arms on a 'military' shield.

*Ornamental cartouches and other shapes* Once the practical use of the shield disappeared, arms began to be displayed on all kinds of ornamental shapes and designs of a perplexing

*RIGHT A ceremonial shield of 15th century Florentine workmanship; note the diapering on the gold background.*

A

B

C

C

D

E

*The achievement of arms of a member of the Drury family, displayed on a stained glass cartouche for hanging in a window.*

*The principal shapes and styles of shields are as follows: **A** the long shield **B** the short or heater-shaped shield **C** the square-shaped shield (shown in two styles) **D** the horsehead shield, and **E** the lozenge.*

variety. Nowadays there has been something of a return to the beginnings of Heraldry, to an earlier, simple style, and a simple shield is now fashionable. The square-shaped shield is used when several different armorial bearings are represented; the oval and the lozenge are still used to display women's Heraldic devices. But it should be made clear that the shape of the shield is not sacred; it can be changed, due consideration being given to style and period, to any shape that best suits the design of the armorial bearings that it displays or the article upon which it is placed. All that matters is that the design conforms to Heraldic ideals and be in good taste.

## THE HELMET

In the days of hand-to-hand warfare adequate protection for the head was provided by a simple iron cap or basinet, which was sufficient to protect the wearer from sword blows. Later a noseplate and cheek plates were added. When cavalry was introduced the helmet had to be much stronger and so the helmet which closed with a visor and which had a plate around the neck — a gorget — was introduced. Helmets with bars and grids across the face were also introduced.

Ceremonial helmets, usually of the type with bars, were made of softened leather and were richly decorated. They were used as vehicles to display the crest, especially in countries where whole families display the same armorial bearings on the shield and identify the individual only by a different crest.

In some countries it is the custom to use dif-

ferent types and posture of helmet, or 'helm' as it is more usually called, to diffentiate men according to this social rank. This, however, is only a custom, not a rule, and it is often broken.

*The pot helm* This, the oldest type of helm, was worn over the top of the small basinet and chain-mail gorget. Its use in Heraldry is limited to gentlemen in Scotland and some families of ancient lineage, in Germany and Denmark.

*The tilting helm* This helm was used by gentlemen and esquires in England, the Scandinavian countries, Germany and Poland, and (though less commonly), by persons of all ranks throughout Europe. Some members of the German, Austrian, Hungarian and Polish nobility have used it to show that their armorial bearings are of more ancient lineage than those depicted by 'newer men' on the more modern barred helm. It is also used in Italian Heraldry for non-titled ranks. Civic and corporate armorial bearings in England usually use this type of helm.

*The helm with open visor and no bars* This type is used, usually facing the front, by British knights and baronets (hereditary knights) and Russian Leibkanpanez.

*The barred helm* This helm, found in a variety of forms and styles, is used all over Europe, usually to denote titled rank, though in Belgium, the Netherlands and Spain it is used by untitled ranks as well. The posture of the helm varies from country to country, and alterations in the number of bars and the artistic treatment are then used to signify distinctions of rank. An English peer of whatever rank, for example, uses a five-barred helm facing to the left (as you look at it). On the Continent this helm, whether facing the front or either side, is used by all ranks. In Italy and Spain the posture, the number of bars and the amount of gold used demonstrate the rank of the bearer. In Denmark and the Netherlands a silver helm is used for non-titled persons, gold for peers.

*The armet* This helm, with the visor open or closed and with or without bars, is used in Italian and Spanish Heraldry and, to a lesser extent, in France. Its style is quite different from that of the other helms used in European Heraldry, so that its use in an Achievement may give a good clue to the bearer's origins.

All the European sovereigns have used gold helms, facing the front and topped by a royal crown. In England the royal helm shows eight bars; others show a gold helm with the visor open.

Although the conventions that govern the use of helms are not rules (despite attempts to standardize the use of helms to indicate the rank of the wearer), there are discernible national styles that should help students to discover the origin and rank of the wearer. But the helm alone is never conclusive evidence; it should be considered with caution and assessed in the context of the style of the other items of the Achievement.

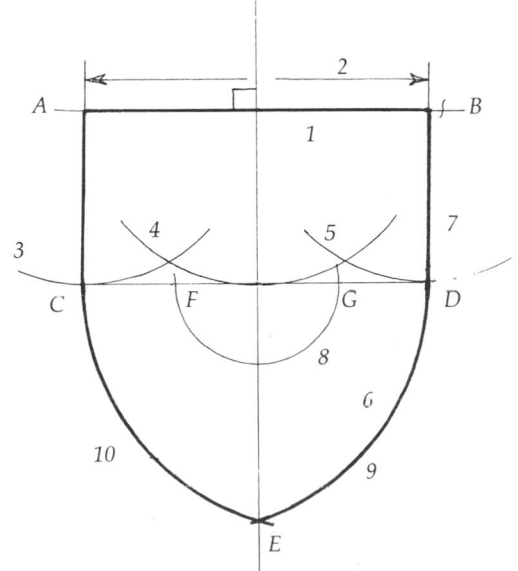

*A simple method for constructing a quartered shield: draw two squares hanging from the line AB and from the points F and G respectively make the two arcs DE and CE. The proportions of the shield can be altered by altering the positions of F and G.*

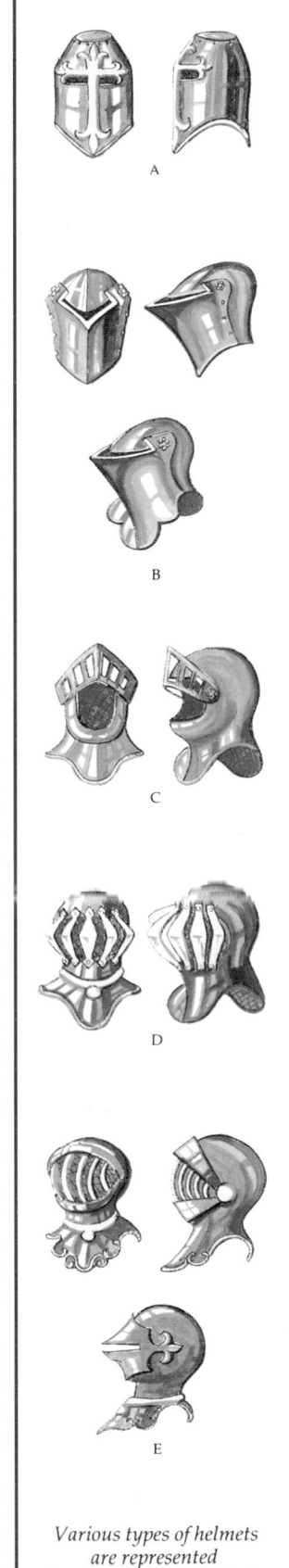

*Various types of helmets are represented here: **A** the pot helm **B** the tilting helm **C** the helm with open visor and no bars **D** the barred helm **E** the armet.*

## THE CREST

It will be seen from looking at any Achievement of Arms that shows a helmet that it is very unusual for the helmet to have nothing placed upon it. Usually a helmet bears a crest. The crest is a product of the tournament, and because of the importance of pageantry and display in a tournament, the crest, which was proudly fixed atop the helm, became increasingly complicated and large. Every kind of emblem, carved of wood or made of leather and stiffened canvas and richly painted and gilded, was devised and the devices chosen were representations of every kind of thing imaginable. Sometimes they repeated the devices on the armorial bearings, or a part of them; often they were any other thing, real or imaginary, that could be contrived to sit securely atop the helm.

In England nowadays the practice is for all members of a family to exhibit the same crest, but there are several instances of unrelated families displaying similar crests, so that the crest is not a reliable emblem of identification. When family ties and tradition are felt to be important, the crest is displayed on its own, especially on items such as rings, silver, china and glass, that are likely to be handed down from one generation to the next.

On the Continent, where families display the same armorial bearings, each member sports a different crest, by which he may be recognized. It is therefore a very personal emblem. It was often the practice, before a tournament, for helmets, with their crests, to be displayed for inspection, especially by ladies of the court. If a lady espied the crest of someone who had in any way wronged any of her number, she would touch the helm and it would be thrown to the floor by a Herald. The owner was not then able to take part in the tournament and there was nothing for it but for him to pick up his helm and slink off in disgrace.

Prince

Duke

Count

Baron

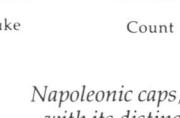
Knight

*Napoleonic caps, each with its distinctive headband and plumage to denote rank, were introduced into republican France by the Emperor Napoleon to dissociate French Heraldry from the abolished monarchy.*

*LEFT A chair-back in the House of Lords, worked in tapestry representing the Royal arms of England; the crest is a lion statant (standing), guardant (front-facing), above a Royal crown on a gold helm with seven bars.*

A

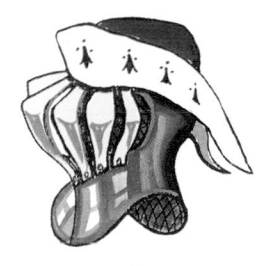

B

C

D

E

F

*A the crest coronet B the chapeau C, D and E the torse or wreath and F the Spanish torse.*

## THE TORSE OR WREATH, THE CHAPEAU, THE CREST CORONET

When it became necessary to modify the rules of the tournament, because so many good men were being killed, one of the new customs was to supply each knight with a club, so that — opponents could strike at one another, mounted on their horses, until the crest of one or the other had been knocked to the ground, and the loser mataphorically toppled into the dust! The crest was secured to the top of the helm as securely as possible and the crude fixings were covered by the following three items.

*The torse or wreath* This is always represented by different coloured materials, twisting together and tied round the helm to cover the gap between the crest and helm. It is thought to have originated from the tournament, when a knight would collect from the crowd a favour from his favourite lady to show that he fought for her honour and as her champion and would tie it round his helm. In Great Britain it now consists of six twists of alternating colour, always with a metal colour (silver or gold) first. On the Continent it is often of five or seven segments, so that a symmetrical design is produced. In Italy a slim torse of ten or twelve sections is used. In Spain, where crests are not used, untitled persons use a plume of ostrich feathers, which are held in place by a torse placed vertically over the crown of the helm. The torse is also used in France, in both forms, and in Holland and Germany.

*The chapeau* In Great Britain, helms are sometimes seen with the crest standing on what appears to be a red cap with a turned-up ermine lining, which is placed over the top of the helm, with no torse. This is a symbol of royal privilege and is seldom encountered. In Scotland, hereditary barons use a blue chapeau as an emblem of their rank.

*The crest coronet* Often found atop a helmet is a crest coronet, in place of the torse, out of which issues the crest. This simple coronet is found throughout Europe and the crest coronet should not be confused with a coronet of rank, which is displayed by peers, princes and sovereigns. It has been used as decorative feature, perhaps to invest the wearer with a dignity that he might otherwise not have. It should be pointed out that Spain and Italy uses coronets of rank with no crest atop the helm, although in Italy the coronet always sits on a narrow torse. Italy, like Spain, does not use crests. Helms with coronets of rank are found in Russian, Polish, Hungarian and Scandinavian Heraldry. Apart from their decorative function, the torse, the wreath and the crest coronet are all designed to hold the mantelling in place on the helm.

Napoleon tried to sweep away all French Heraldry associated with royalty and introduced a new system. In the place of helmets and crests a series of black caps, known as Napoleonic caps, each with different plumes and headbands, was introduced to indicate rank.

## MANTELLING OR LAMBREQUIN

When the Crusaders went to free the Holy Land, fitted out with all the weaponry, armour and accoutrements of war of medieval knights, they soon discovered that they were ill equipped to fight in a hot, dusty and arid climate. They rapidly adopted the native practice of wearing a small cloak or cloth fastened to the top of the helm to keep the sun off their backs. That covering became known as the mantelling. It became fashionable for knights to have their mantelling slashed to pieces, to show that they had been in many fierce battles. This custom accounts for the fantastic designs and shapes of mantelling that may be encountered, from the simple, restrained kerchief hanging at the back of the helm (usually seen with a pot helm) to the wildly extravagant swirls and masses that have become so exaggerated that they have earned the description 'mass of seaweed'.

It is usual for the mantelling to be of two colours, the principal metal colour of the armorial bearings on the inside and on the outside the principal colour. In describing mantelling the outside colour is always mentioned first, and then the inside, describing the latter as 'turned or doubled', whichever it may be. It is not unusual to find mantelling of two or more outside colours, nor to find them turned, doubled or lined with a fur, or with metals of different colours. You may find the outside strewn with devices, sometimes echoing those displayed on the shield, or find them covered with badges. Sometimes, when the crest is an animal or person, the mantelling is a continuation of the skin of the animal or the vesture of the person.

## THE USE OF MORE THAN ONE HELM AND CREST

When different armorial Achievements become invested in one person, it is quite common to find more than one helm and crest used on an Achievement; in German Heraldry as many as twelve may be used. In Great Britain, where it is unusual to find more than three, it is the practice to place all the helms facing the dexter. On the Continent they are placed to respect each other, the most important on the dexter side, or in the middle if there are more than two.

## CORONETS OF RANK

In the Achievements of peers, it is common to find displayed between the shield and the helms the coronet of rank. This is common practice in most European countries, except Spain, Portugal and Italy, where no crest is used and the coronet is placed on the helm. It is also common for peers simply to display a shield showing their armorial devices and their coronets of rank. It is important not to confuse coronets of rank with crest coronets or Heraldic crowns.

## INSIGNIA OF OFFICE

It is quite common for insignia denoting some office held by the bearer of the Achievement — such as the two crossed batons of the Earl Marshal of England — to be placed behind the shield.

ANCIENT DESIGN

FANCIFUL ELABORATION

MODERN DESIGN

*Three designs of mantelling.*

PRINCE

DUKE

EARL

MARQUIS

VISCOUNT

BARON

*Each rank of the English nobility has its own coronet, as illustrated here.*

RIGHT *The armorial bearings of Sir Ronald Gardner-Thorpe show the circlet of a Knight of the British Empire, with the badge of the order on the ribbons below, and the Cross of the order of the Knights of St John.*

## THE CHAINS, MEDALS & CROSSES OF ORDERS OF CHIVALRY

It is not uncommon to find placed behind the shield a cross of an order of chivalry, which denotes that the bearer is a knight commander of the relevant order. Ribands of chivalric orders of knighthood, with the motto of the order on them, are also found encircling shields. Knights of the order may encircle their riband with the chain collar of the order. Badges or decorations, of an order, in the lesser ranks, may be hung below the shield, shown suspended from ribands.

## SUPPORTERS

On many Achievements of Arms the shield and the helm sometimes appear as if they were held up by two animals or other beings, acting as supporters. This practice emanates from the earliest Heraldic times and is thought to have been begun by seal engravers, filling in the space between the side of the engraved shield and the round edge of the seal with mythical beasts such as small dragons. The practice of using supporters probably became widespread with the rise of the tournament at which knights employed their pages to parade around the arena, carrying their masters' shields and dressed in fantastic costumes, to the delight of the crowd.

Supporters may take any form, from animals or humans to mythical or celestial beings. It is more usual to find two supporters, one on each side, although frequently only one is used.

The use of supporters varies greatly from country to country and care should be taken not to confuse supporters that are properly part of the Achievement of Arms with those that have been added purely for artistic effect.

In Great Britain, supporters may be granted by the appropriate authority as part of the Achievement of Arms and handed down from father to son. They may be used by peers, senior ranks of some civic authorities and corporate bodies. The same is true in Scotland, where their controlled use is also extended to some barons and clan chiefs. In the Netherlands there are no restrictions on their use. In Germany and Austria they are used only by the higher ranks of the peerage; but there is no definite rule and peers quite often do not use them. It is common for the national arms of this area, and those of its sovereigns and princes, to use one supporter, the eagle, in its many forms, with the shield displayed on the breast. Italy, Spain and Portugal generally do not use supporters. In Belgium their use is generally confined to the nobility and to some civic authorities.

Supporters can be two identical beings or two that are completely dissimilar. They may be carrying any kind of weapon or banner or any

*The three Coats of Arms shown here are **A** the arms of Baron Manvers **B** the arms of the Duke of Argyll (showing the emblem of the Hereditary Grand Master of the Household and Hereditary Justice-General of Scotland), and **C** the arms of the Earl Marshal of England (showing the batons of office and the blue ribbon of the Garter).*

RIGHT *An achievement of arms with griffin supporters.*

*The Achievement of Arms of the Borough of Beccles follows the usual practice of including two supporters.*

# Griffin

The griffin is the king of all the creatures. Whilst the lion is the king of the beasts and the eagle is the king of the birds, the griffin that bears a combination of the best attributes of both these magnificent creatures, like a good claret, is better than the sum of its constituent parts. Its amalgamation gains in courage and boldness. Its fierceness and strength are increased. It is used to denote strength and military courage and leadership. It is composed of the head, neck and fore feet of an eagle, with the body, back legs and tail of a lion. The female is drawn with wings and the male with tusks on its lower beak and spines emanating from its back.

FEMALE GRIFFIN

MALE GRIFFIN

# Supporters

Supporters and their artistic treatment offer the artist the most scope. They must conform to the correct heraldic posture and tincture but they have great flexibility with regard to style and in the design of the whole achievement, allowing a balanced composition to be designed that is both fitting for the shape of the space available and which reflects the style of the time in which it was rendered.

They are interesting in the amazing variety of creature that is employed. Every kind of mythical and real creature is brought into use and can be found bearing their master's arms with pride across the pages of history. Lord Twinning uses a crested crane and a giraffe. Cobbold has two yellow labradors. Freyberg two salamanders proper (a salamander proper is depicted bright red and in flames). These were no doubt used as an illusion to the name. The City of Inverness uses an elephant and camel and Australia uses a kangaroo and an emu.

There are numerous examples of lions, stags, hounds of many different kinds and horses, some of which are mounted. Lord Birdwood employs dexter a Sergeant of the XII Bengal Lancers mounted on a bay horse and sinister a Sikh Daffador of XI Bengal Lancers mounted on a chestnut horse, both habited and accoutred proper. Bulls, bears, wolves and boars are commonly found. Even the tiny ermine and its larger cousin the otter.

The mythical creatures appear in equal array. Dragons and griffins are commonly used and so is the wyvern. Lord Arbuthnot uses two wyverns, vert, their tails nowed (knotted together) vomiting flames proper. Heraldic panthers, antelopes, yale and tigers appear. (For information about all these creatures, see the section on the mythical creatures).

Human beings are used in every variety. Serving officers tend to show supporters of the units with which they served. Lord Baden Powell had an officer of the 13th/18th Hussars, his sword drawn over his shoulder and a boy Scout holding a staff proper, representing the Regiment with which he served and the world famous youth movement that he founded. Admiral Lord Fisher uses on either side a sailor of the Royal Navy supporting an anchor, cabled all proper. The Worshipful Company of Farmers bears on either side a farmworker proper. Both these achievements used supports dressed as of the time when they were granted. Uniform and dress has changed over the years. A farmworker drawn now might more properly be depicted in Wellington boots, a green overall, rubber gloves and a spray hood! It is important for the heraldic artist to bear these differences in mind and as far as possible illustrate such things in the costume of the period of the original grant, if this can be ascertained. It is quite common to find clerics of different denominations and sometimes saints. Wild men or savages are fairly commonly employed, depicted as naked, with a wreath of leaves about the loin and head and usually wielding a large club. Women also appear, as serving members of nursing or military units, or simply as

THE ARMORIAL BEARINGS OF THE WORSHIPFUL COMPANY OF FARMWORKERS

THE ARMORIAL BEARINGS OF THE WORSHIPFUL COMPANY OF FISHMONGERS

maidens, more or less dressed. The Worshipful Company of Needlemakers use a representation of Adam and Eve wreathed about the waist with fig leaves, sewn proper. The Worshipful Company of Glaziers has on either side a boy proper holding in the exterior hand a torch or, inflamed proper. These boys are always drawn naked as no mention is made of their vesture. Of the human monsters and mythical beings, angels appear quite often. An angel is supposed to be shown sexless and it is not really correct to draw it as a nubile young female, as is sometimes seen. They are usually shown in a long straight gown, with just feet and hands visible, long fair hair and wings. Those fearful creatures, the harpies are used as supporters and so too are mermaids, mermen or tritons. The Worshipful Company of Fishmongers bears dexter a merman holding in his right hand a falchoin (a type of sea axe) sinister a mermaid holding in her left hand a mirror, all proper. Mermaids are very vain and beautiful beings and are shown with a mirror and usually a comb. Sir Harry Secombe bears as a charge a mermaid combing her hair (sea comb) and has a motto in English which says 'Go on'. Such elegant and simple blazonry embodies the spirit and imagination that is the very essence of heraldry.

Birds too play an important part as supporters and eagles and falcons abound. The Spectacle Makers have two falcons (keen sight). The Emperors of the Holy Roman Empire used one double-headed eagle, displayed (to show dominion over east and west) and charged their arms upon its breast. As with animals, all kinds of birds are used. Ostriches, lyre birds, parrots, albatrosses, doves and condors. Even two mallard, larks and goldfinches. The Scrivener's Company have two secretary birds. Lord Brabazon bears so elegantly on either side, supporting the shield in its beak, a gull volant (flying) over water, proper. Even fish are enrolled in this noble task. Lord Temnart bears two dolphins proper and the City of Glasgow bears on either side a salmon hurient, bearing in its mouth a ring or, enjewled gules. This is in honour of the legend of St Kentergern who came there and worked many miracles, one of which was to restore Queen Rederech's lost ring to her with the aid of a salmon. As well as all the beings of creation and of myth and imagination, some inanimate objects have been employed. The City of Southampton uses on either side on the quarter-deck of a two-masted sailing vessel on the sea, proper, a lion rampant or. Lord Boyd Orr uses two wheat sheaves.

other object appropriate to the bearer. Flying birds are sometimes used, or two ships.

It is perfectly permissible to show armorial bearings that should have supporters without them; for although they may form part of a grant of armorial bearings they are, like everything else but the shield, not essential elements of an Achievements.

## THE MANTEAU OR ROBE OF ESTATE AND PAVILION

Princes, the higher representatives of the nobility and certain high officials of secular bodies or the Church display their whole Achievements upon a representation of a draped cloak, usually with a colour outside and one of the furs within. There are many varieties of this custom, though it is not practised in Great Britain.

## THE COMPARTMENT

In most instances it is felt that the supporters should have something to stand upon and this is know as the compartment. (though there are plenty of examples of Achievements with supporters left hanging in the air, as is were, without compartments). The compartment may consist of almost anything. It may represent solid ground (often strewn with herbage or flowers, or badges), water or simply ornamental scroll work. A motto riband is sometimes used.

## THE MOTTO

Mottoes are found in many Achievements. In Scotland they are regarded as an essential ingredient and are placed on a riband above the helm. In England, as on the Continent, they are not regarded as part of the Achievement, but they may, if desired, be placed below the shield. The riband is usually drawn as ornately as the style and period allow and is usually shown white outside and of a colour on the reverse.

## BADGES

It is quite common to find a badge as part of an Achievement. A badge is a simple Heraldic device that belongs to the bearer, but which other people can wear to show their allegiance to him or his cause. A badge would be worn by the retainers, messengers and soldiers of the bearer. In the days when knights held tenure of their lands in exchange for military service, they would come to the battle in their own coat of arms, but also displaying the badge of their overlord. Badges survive today and are worn by military units, fire brigades, police forces, schools and universities and the like.

Badges are sometimes arranged into the composition of an Achievement, so as to be included with it but not form part of it; they may also be found strewn on the compartment or mantelling.

ABOVE *Badges of the St John family on the tomb of Nicholas St John;* TOP LEFT *the sun in splendour,* CENTRE *a fetlock.*

LEFT *A stone carving by S & J Winter illustrates the use of a single supporter in Heraldry.*

BELOW LEFT *The armorial bearings of the Chelmsford Borough Council, engraved by Stefan Oliver, have an unusual compartment, consisting of a bridge over water, retained by a motto riband.*

*The banners of the present Knights of the Garter, in St George's Chapel, Windsor.*

RIGHT *The banner of the present Knights of the Bath in the Henry VII chapel, Westminster Abbey.*

ABOVE FAR RIGHT *The Turberville window in Bere Regis Church in Dorset; the* Turberville arms are impaled with their many spouses.

BELOW FAR RIGHT *The arms of Sir William Clopton (1591–1618) impaling those of his first wife, Anne, daughter of Sir Thomas Barnadiston.*

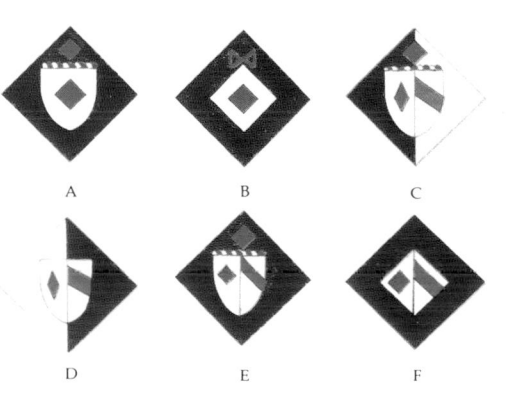

*Shown here are the hatchments of **A** a dead bachelor **B** a dead spinster **C** a dead husband **D** a dead wife **E** a dead widower, and **F** a dead widow.*

# FLAGS

Many different flags are used in Heraldry, their main purpose being to display the Heraldic bearings of their owners, to advertise their presence or to serve as a rallying-point for men in battle.

## —— BANNERS ——

Historically banners are square and display the bearer's arms upon them, as they would be seen on his coat, armour and shield. Fine examples of these can be seen in St. George's Chapel, Windsor, and Westminster Abbey, where the banners of the present Knights of the Garter and Knights of the Bath, respectively, hang. Any armigerous person can have a banner and fly it from his house when he is present. Banners can also be rectangular, both vertically and horizontally, though in modern parlance the latter shape is generally called a flag. Nowadays most national banners are flag-shaped, like the English Royal Banner, which is universally but quite wrongly called the Royal Standard.

Banners were also used at sea with long streamers of the livery colours. It has been known for arms to be emblazoned on the sails of ships. The Admiral of England in 1436 was the Earl of Huntingdon, who bore on his mainsail the motto, 'England within a bordure of France'. (A bordure is a narrow band running along the edge of a shield.)

## —— PENNONS ——

The pennon was a small triangular flag carried at the tip of a spear by a knight, showing his personal device. It was made so that the arms were displayed the right way when he was charging and the spear was level.

## —— LIVERY COLOURS ——

It was the custom of those persons who had retainers to dress them in a uniform so that they could be easily recognized. These uniforms were usually of two colours, usually, though not universally, the chief colour and metal of the bearer's arms. The Tudor kings of England had green and white as their livery colours.

## —— STANDARDS ——

A standard is a long narrow flag; the longer the flag, the higher the rank of the bearer. It is simply a device for display and pageant, used to present the devices and the livery colour of the bearer.

Though the items displayed on standards have varied in the past, nowadays standards show the arms of the bearer next to the pole. The rest of the standard is divided horizontally into the two livery colours. On this is shown the crest, perhaps repeated, the motto on a riband placed diagonally in as many pieces as are needed and any badge that may be granted. Standards, like badges, are granted by the relevant Heraldic authority to any armigerous person.

## —— MILITARY COLOURS ——

Military units of all kinds have traditionally carried into battle a banner displaying their badge, their sovereign allegiance and details of their history and battles. Military colours have always been treated with great respect representing as they do the glories and traditions of the regiment. For this reason the colours have been defended with unsurpassed valour in numerous battles. These colours are still proudly displayed today.

# HATCHMENTS

It is quite important to mention hatchments, as they are frequently found in churches, often without any explanation of their meaning.

It used to be the custom to paint the Coat of Arms of an armiger on a board and hang it up outside his house when he died. This painting would then be carried to the church at the funeral and afterwards hung there for all time. In the days before newspapers this was the most practical way of letting everyone know that someone had died. The Achievement was always placed on a diamond board and the style of the composition indicated which member of the household had died. The clue, apart from the Heraldic accoutrements, lay in the background of the board, which was painted black behind the arms of the deceased.

CHAPTER FIVE

# *Armorial Bearings*

HE SHIELD is the one indispensable part of an Achievement. It now bears the armorial bearings of a person, which would otherwise be borne on his Coat of Arms, horse trappings, flags, banners, sail or what you will. It is from the Coat of Arms that we derive the name now used to describe the shield, and what is displayed on it. In modern parlance this has been shortened simply to 'arms'. One applies to the appropriate Heraldic authority for a grant of 'arms' (short for 'armorial bearings'). At the same time the other items to be included in the Achievement, as appropriate to the applicant's rank and circumstances, are assigned. The term, 'Coat of Arms', therefore, has become synonymous with the shield and what is displayed upon it. All modern designs of armorial bearings are prepared with a view to their being displayed upon a shield; and it is therefore im-portant to understand what is displayed, since these symbols and emblems are the mainstay of Heraldry.

## THE BLAZON

A written description of a Coat of Arms may at first appear to make little sense; but once you become used to the language and the way that it is set out, you will find that a well-written de-scription is a masterpiece of concision that should enable any artist to draw correctly every-thing that is displayed on the shield. This de-scription is known as the 'blazon'. To 'blazon' a coat of arms is to describe it in words. To 'emblazon' it, is to paint or draw it in full colour. Because the blazon always follows a set pattern, we will consider what might be painted on a shield in the same order.

*BELOW Ancient examples of Coats of Arms bearing a plain tincture only are (from left to right) those of Bruget of Normandy ('argent'), Berrington of Chester ('azure') and the Duke of Brittany ('ermine').*

## DIVISION OF THE FIELD

PER PALE

PER SALTIRE

QUARTERLY

GYRONY

MASONY

*As the number of gentlemen bearing arms increased, single-tincture Coats of Arms were no longer sufficient, despite the variety of charges placed upon them, to distinguish one from another. Two coloured shields were therefore introduced. Illustrated here and overleaf are the various methods of dividing a shield.*

PER PALE

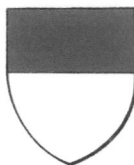

PER FESSE

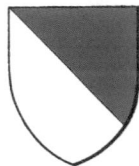

PER BEND

PER BEND SINISTER

PER CHEVRON

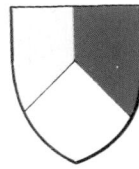

TIERCED IN PAIRLE

## THE FIELD

Before any design is placed on a shield, the shield is painted a colour, which can be one of the metals, colours or furs. There are examples of Coats of Arms that consisted of a plain tincture only. Bruget of Normandy bore a Coat of Arms and a shield 'argent' (silver or white), the Duke of Brittany bore 'ermine' and Berrington of Chester bore 'azure'. Notwithstanding all the things imaginable that might be placed on a blue shield, for example, it was soon necessary for differentiation to use two-coloured shields, with one half red, say, and the other white.

*A field semy, semé, strewn or powdered* Sometimes a field will be found strewn with many small charges and these are usually of a stated colour. Some of them have their own special terms:
'Semy de lis' or 'semy of fleur de lis' means 'representing the lily', while 'crusiley' means that the field is strewn with little crosses. Other terms are 'of the roundels', 'pomme', 'bezanty', 'platy', 'of the guttés' and 'gutté d'or'.

*The divisions of the field* The shield can be divided in a variety of ways and the form of the division and the colours to be used are always mentioned first in the blazon. Each different form of division of the field, has its own term, each of which is illustrated below. When describing a divided field, the colour in the top dexter corner is always given first.

*The lines of partition* In all the examples shown, the divisions are made with straight lines. They can, however, be made with a variety of zigzag or wavy lines, which are shown below. In a blazon the order of description is as follows: the division of the field (if any), the configuration of the line (if not straight) and the colours, the top dexter being first.

## THE CHARGES

Any item placed upon the field of the shield is known as a charge. If a shield has anything placed on it, it is said to be charged with that object. Similarly a lion with a rose on its shoulder is described as being 'charged on the shoulder with a rose'.

It has become the custom in an illustration of a Coat of Arms to show any charge placed upon the field as casting a shadow. As well as enhancing the artistic effect, the shadow shows that the item is not part of the field, but is 'charged' upon it. The light is always shown as coming from the dexter top. The provision of a shadow is, however, by no means a rule and in small works it is frequently omitted for the sake of clarity. Charges of all kinds can themselves be charged in never-ending successions and combinations.

*The ordinaries* This main group of charges consists of geometric shapes placed upon a shield, stripes in different combinations and other shapes. An ordinary usually takes up about one-third of the area of the shield. It is import-

BARRY

BENDY

BENDY SINISTER

PALY

LOZENGY

CHEQUEY

## LINES OF PARTITION

DANCY

DOVETAILED

EMBATTLED

ENARCHED

ENGRAILED

FLORY/COUNTER-FLORY

INDENTED

NEBULY

POTENTY

RAGULY

RAYONNÉ

WAVY

WREATHY

URDY

*Lines of partition may be drawn in a great number of ways, as illustrated here.*

## SOME EXAMPLES OF LINES OF PARTITION

A FESS DANCY

A BEND WAVY

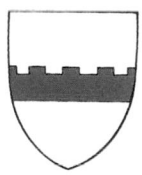
A FESSE EMBATTLED

A PALE INDENTED

A SALTIRE ENGRAILED

THREE BENDLETS ENHANCED

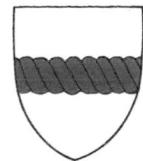
A FESSE WREATHY

*Various ways in which lines of partition may divide a shield are illustrated here.*

LEFT *An achievement of arms of one of the many armigerous Smith families, showing argent on a fess nebuly counter-nebuly sable three rabbits' heads erased argent, in the second and third quarters.*

ORDINARIES

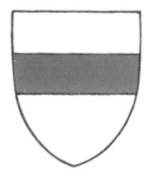

FESSE

PALL

BEND

PILE

BEND SINISTER

SALTIRE

CHEVRON

COMPONY

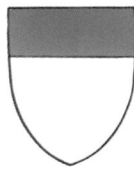

CHIEF

COUNTER COMPONY

CROSS

CHEQUEY

PALE

*The principal ordinaries are illustrated here.*

ant to remember that an ordinary is not a division of the field, but a charge placed upon it. All the main ordinaries are illustrated.

*The sub-ordinaries* These are smaller geometric charges, less frequently used, but no less important. These too can soon be learned and, once remembered, are easily recognized.

*The roundels and gutté* The roundels appear as different coloured circles each with their own name. A gold roundel is a bezant, a silver roundel is called a plate, red, a torteau, blood-red, a guze, blue, a hurt, green, a pomme, black, a pellate, ogress or gunstone, purple a golpe, orange, an orange, and when barry, wavy, argent and azure, a fountain.

'Gutté' (or 'gutty', 'goutty') means 'strewn with droplets'. Like the roundels, they have a different name for each colour. Care should be taken not to confuse these with the many forms of ermine spot. 'Gutté d'or' describes a field or charge strewn with gold drops, 'gutté d'eau' silver drops, 'gutté de sang', red drops, 'gutté des larmes', blue drops, 'de poix', black drops, and 'd'huile' (or more rarely, 'd'olive') green drops.

*Combinations* Combinations of these groups are frequently seen and a few examples are set out below.

*Counterchanging* This very attractive feature is quite often encountered and it presents some impossible-looking combinations of shape and colour until the idea is mastered: a charge is placed over a divided field and the colours are reversed. Some exciting and exotic effects can be produced by this very simple method, some examples of which are shown so that you will recognize it when you see it.

*Other charges* Any object may be placed upon a shield either on its own or in combination with the ordinaries, sub-ordinaries, or other unrelated objects. Charges may be of any colour, including their own natural colour, and they may be counter-changed with the field or the ordinaries or be themselves charged with other charges. The variety is endless, and needs to be, to ensure that each Coat of Arms is unique. The only limitations are those imposed by good taste and the rule of tincture concerning the use of colour, metal and fur.

*Canting arms* Mention has several times been made of charges that relate to the name of the bearer. This was a very common practice and is still carried on wherever possible. Unfortunately, with the change of language, the meaning of the allusion has often been lost.

MOLLET

BILLET

SUB-ORDINARIES

TWO BARS

TWO BARS GEMEL

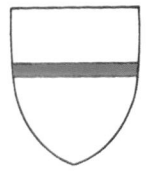

BARRULET

BATON

TWO BENDLET

GYRON

LABEL

## SUB-ORDINARIES

BORDURE

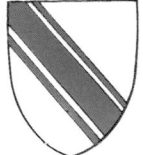

CANTON

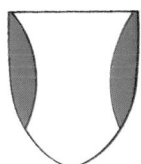

THREE CHEVRONELS

BEND COTTISED

FLAUNCHES

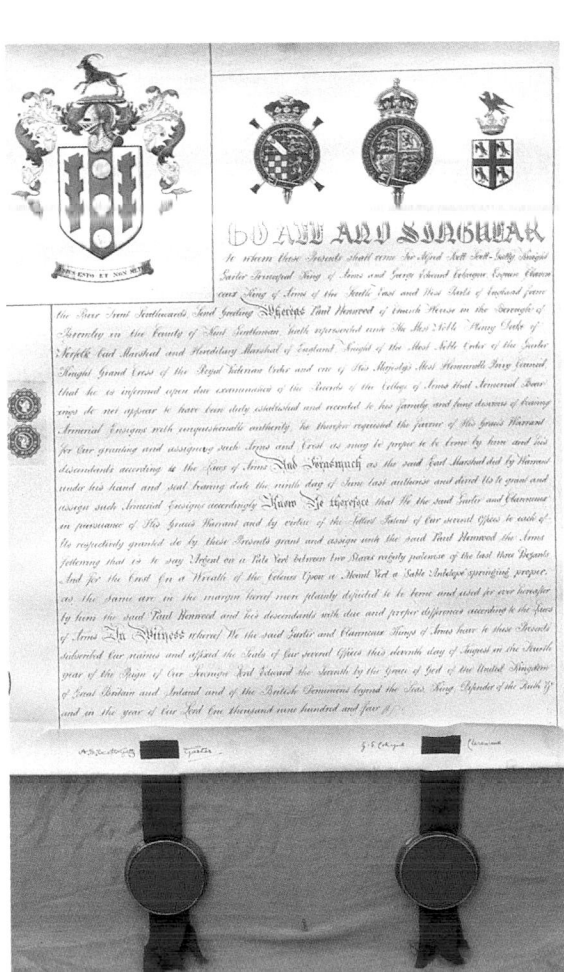

D'OR (GOLD)

D'EAU (WHITE)

DE SANG (RED)

DES LARMES (BLUE)

DE POIX (BLACK)

DE HUILE (GREEN)

GUTTÉ DROPLETS

# DESCRIBING A SHIELD

There are two ways, apart from painting or drawing a detailed picture of the Coat of Arms, in which it may be described.

The first, (as has already been briefly mentioned), is the blazon. It is quite tricky to master, until you get the hang of it. All blazons follow a set pattern. Firstly they describe the divisions of the field, if there are any, and the partition lines, if they are not straight. They consider next the main charge, then any secondary charges that may be placed either side of the main charge, and next any other charges that may be placed on the main charge.

Practice with a published armorial (to be found in most libraries) is a good way to develop the knack.

The second is a method known as 'the trick'. This is a shorthand method of annotating a Coat of Arms – the sort of note that might be made to serve as a reminder of a Coat of Arms seen, say, on a public building, in order to identify it later. This is the main use for the abbreviations found in Heraldry and they are very quickly learned.

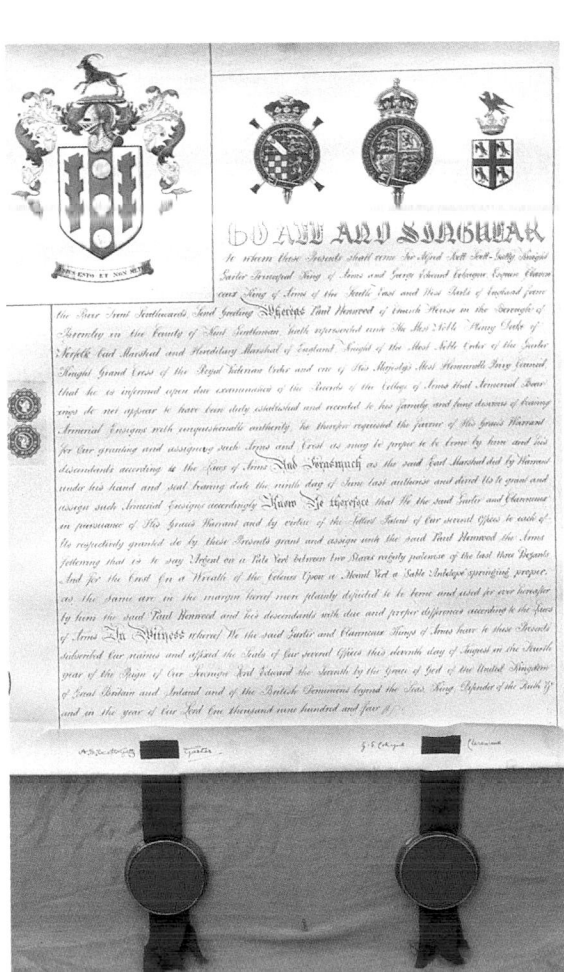

*ABOVE The grant of arms of the Henwood family of Kent; such documents conferring arms are issued in the same form by the Heralds of England and Scotland to the present day.*

## SUB-ORDINARIES

CROSS FIMBRIATED

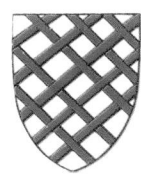

FRET

FRETTY

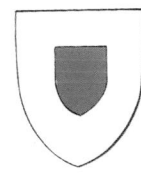

ESQUIRE

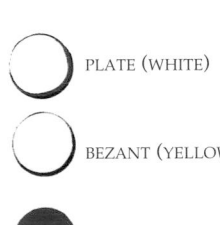

ESCUTCHEON

PLATE (WHITE)

BEZANT (YELLOW)

TORTEAU (RED)

HURT (BLUE)

PELLATE, OGRESS, GUNSTONE (BLACK)

ROUNDELS

## SUB-ORDINARIES

ORLE

CROSS QUARTER-PIERCED

TRESSURE

DOUBLE TRESSURE

CROSS VOIDED

ORANGE (ORANGE)

POMME (GREEN)

GOLPE (PURPLE)

FOUNTAIN (BLUE & WHITE)

ROUNDELS

| SUB-ORDINARIES | EXAMPLES OF COMBINATIONS | EXAMPLES OF COUNTER-CHANGING | SOME CANTING ARMS | STEPS OF A BLAZON |
|---|---|---|---|---|

FUSIL

LOZENGE

RUSTRE

MASCLE

ANNULET

*Among the sub-ordinaries are included some abstract shapes.*

A

B

C

D

*Four combinations of ordinaries and sub-ordinaries are illustrated here: A argent a fesse between two chevrons gules (Fitzwalter) B per pale azure and gules overall a bend or (Langton) C argent two chevrons with a bordure gules (Albini), and D argent a saltire and chief gules (Bruce).*

A

B

C

D

*Counter-changing may be done in a number of ways. Illustrated here are four examples: A per chevron argent and gules overall a crescent counter-changed (Barker) B per pale argent and gules overall a bend counter-changed (Chaucer) C argent a pile and a chevron counter-changed, and D per pale or and gules a chevron counter-changed (Chambers)*

A

B

C

D

*These four illustrations are examples of canting arms: A argent between three calves sable a fesse gules (Calverly) B argent a squirrel gules eating a gold nut (Squires) C azure three hedgehogs argent (Harris), and D argent between three moorcocks a chevron sable (Moore).*

A

B

C

D

*A shield has four main elements to be described in a blazon: A the colour of the shield (azure) B the main charges (on a chevron) C the secondary charges (between three billets argent), and D any additional charges (three torteaux).*

## CHAPTER SIX

# The Animal Kingdom

O'F ALL the charges used in Heraldry animals and monsters stick most in people's minds. They are extensively used on shields, crests and badges as well as serving as supporters. Beasts always face the dexter when used as a charge, crest or badge, unless otherwise stated, and they always look where they are going, that is to the dexter, again unless otherwise stated. The tail is usually shown erect and curved, in a style according to custom or the discretion of the artist, unless otherwise stated.

There are a number of terms that apply to all animals and monsters collectively classified as beasts.

ARMED When applied to beasts, the term 'armed' refers to beaks, claws, tusks, horns and the like. The term usually occurs when these are of a different colour from the beast itself, as in 'a lion rampant sable, armed gules'.

AFFRONTY Facing the front.

BICORPORATE OR TRICORPORATE One head with two or three bodies.

CRINED With a mane or head of hair, separately tinctured.

COWED With the tail down between the legs.

DEMI The top half of the body only, usually with tail included.

DISARMED With no beak, claws, horns or tusks.

DOUBLE-QUEUED With two tails.

GUARDANT Looking at the observer, full-faced, directly out of the shield.

GORGED With the neck or gorge encircled (by a coronet, for example).

HORNED OR TUSKED In *armed*, above.

LANGUED With a tongue of a specified colour.

NOWED Tied in a knot, usually of the tail.

QUEUE FOURCHY OR FOURCHÉE With a forked tail.

REGARDANT looking backwards.

SINISTER Facing the other way, to the sinister, as in 'a lion rampant sinister'.

TUFTED With tufts of hair.

UNGULED Of the hoofs of an animal, when their colour is different from the colour of the body, as in 'unicorn argent, unguled or'.

VULNED Wounded and bleeding.

*A lion* guardant *has its face towards the viewer.*

*A lion double-queued has two tails.*

*A forked tail is called a* queue fourchy.

*A lion looking backwards is called* regardant.

TOP *A lion* demi *is drawn with the top half of the body only, but usually including the tail.*

ABOVE *A lion* couchant *is drawn lying down in an alert posture.*

*ABOVE The tomb of Richard Berghersh in Lincoln Cathedral; the first and second shields show a lion queue fourchée (with a forked tail). The shield of the Suffolk branch of the family was argent (white), a chief gules (with a red top section covering one third of the shield), overall a lion rampant queue fourchée or.*

*An animal facing the front and cut off cleanly below the ears is described as caboshed.*

*Each of the animals on this badge is described as face, meaning with a head caboshed.*

*An animal facing the side and cut off cleanly behind the ears is described as couped close.*

*Couped is the term for any limb cut off the body cleanly.*

*Erased describes any limb drawn as if torn from the body.*

## —— PARTS OF THE BODY ——

The head and limbs are frequently found as crests, charges and badges and these have special descriptions.

*CABOSHED* Facing the front and cut off cleanly behind the ears.

*COUPED CLOSE* Facing the side and cut off cleanly behind the ears.

*COUPED* Cut off close at the neck.

*ERASED* As if pulled off, with jagged skin.

*FACE* A head caboshed.

*JESSANT DE LIS* A face with a fleur-de-lis behind and thrust out through the mouth.

*LIMBS* Paws, arms, legs and tails are shown couped (cut off close to the body), or erased.

*This illustration shows a face jessant de lis, with a fleur-de-lis behind, coming through the mouth.*

*The limb on the left is couped; the one on the right is erased.*

*Two lions walking in opposite directions are said to be* counter passant.

*Two lions leaping in opposite directions are said to be* counter salient.

*A lion at rest is* dormant.

*Small lions charged on a shield are called lioncells.*

## —— THE ANIMALS ——

Of all the animals the lion is the king. Favoured for his nobility and fierceness, the lion has been used in Heraldry all over the world. He is always displayed looking as fierce and as haughty as the artist can contrive, with his claws extended. His claws and tongue are always painted red, regardless of what colour he is, unless he is on a red field, when they are painted blue. The lion is always shown in one of a variety of set postures, which also apply to other animals. There are a number of terms to describe these postures.

*COUCHANT* Lying down in an alert posture.

*COUNTER PASSANT* Two lions walking in opposite directions.

*COUNTER SALIENT* Two lions leaping in opposite directions.

*DORMANT* Lying down at rest.

*LIONCELLS* Small lions, usually in large numbers on a shield.

*PASSANT* Walking across the shield. A lion 'passant guardant' is known as a leopard; a leopard of England is a 'lion passant guardant or'.

*RAMPANT* Rearing up in fight.

*SALIENT* Taking a leap across the shield.

*SEJANT* Sitting on his haunches. When he sits facing the front he is termed 'affronty'.

*STATANT* Just standing there.

*TWO LIONS ADDORSED* Two lions rampant, back to back.

*TWO LIONS RESPECTANT OR COMBATANT* Two lions rampant, face to face.

Lions are frequently found as supporters in which case they stand holding the shield and, sometimes, the helm as well.

It is common to find the head, arm or paw used as a charge.

It is also common to find lions with collars and chains or with crowns, or carrying something in their paws, or charged on the shoulder with some device. Sometimes they are powdered all over with small charges. There are numerous lion monsters and of these the winged lion and the sea lion are the most common. A lion with a human face and human body and head is also found.

Most animals are found in Heraldry and since the opening up of the New World all kinds of species unknown to earlier Heraldry have been introduced. All of them may appear as supporters, charges or on crests. Some of the most ancient and most common are worth noting.

**BEAR** He is usually shown standing upright on his back legs, holding a tree trunk, and often with a muzzle (derived, no doubt, from the performing bears at medieval fairs and emblematic of having tamed the savage beast).

**BEAVER** He is occasionally found, usually as a symbol of industry.

**BOAR** In medieval times the wild boar was common throughout Europe and regularly hunted. He is a ferocious animal when roused and many people have been killed by his ripping tusks. He

*A lion walking across a shield is* passant; *when it is also looking at the observer (passant guardant) it is known as a leopard.*

*A lion rearing up is* rampant.

*Salient describes an animal leaping across a shield.*

*A lion on its haunches is* sejant.

*A lion simply standing, motionless, is described as* statant.

*Two lions rampant, back-to-back, are called* addorsed.

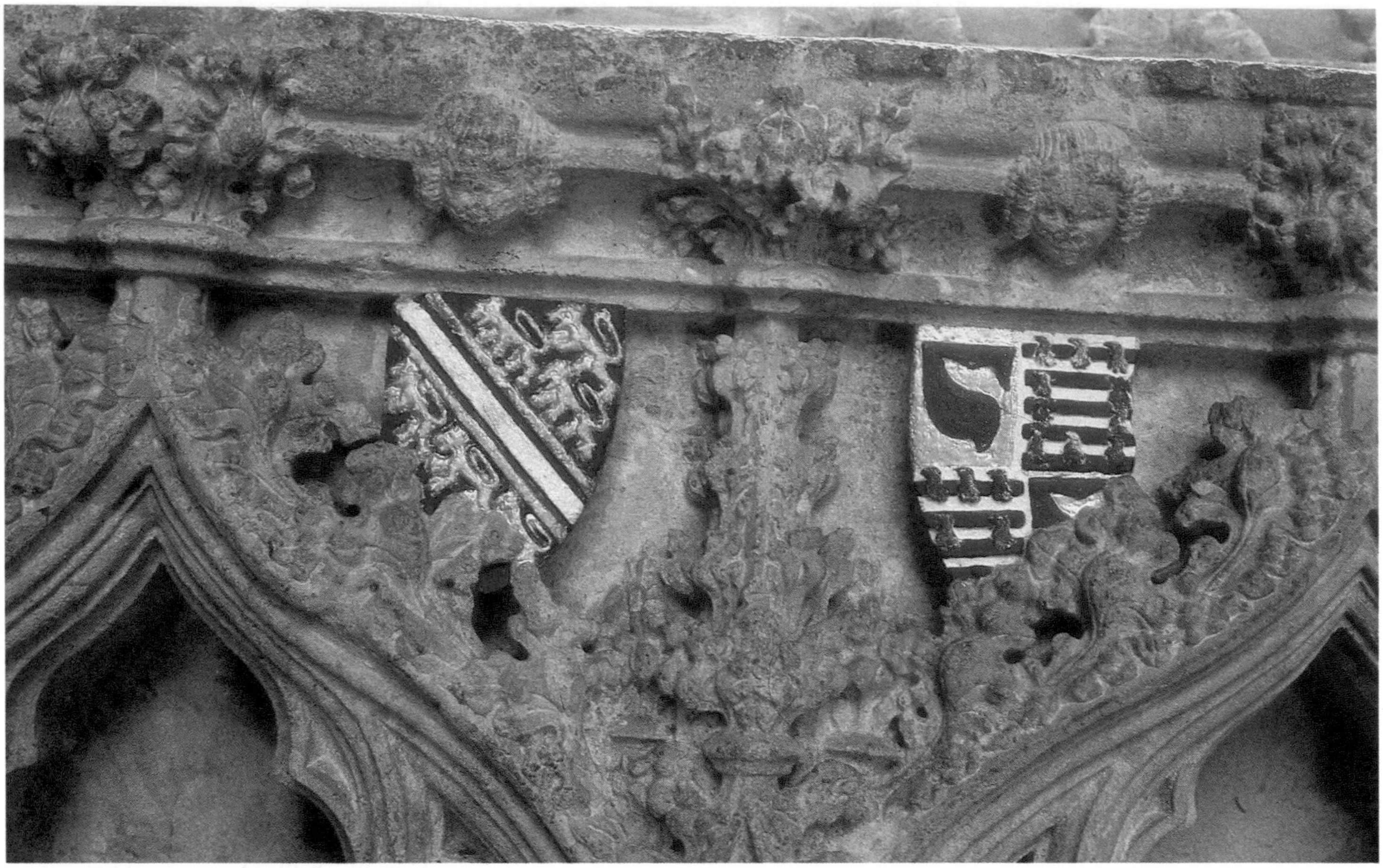

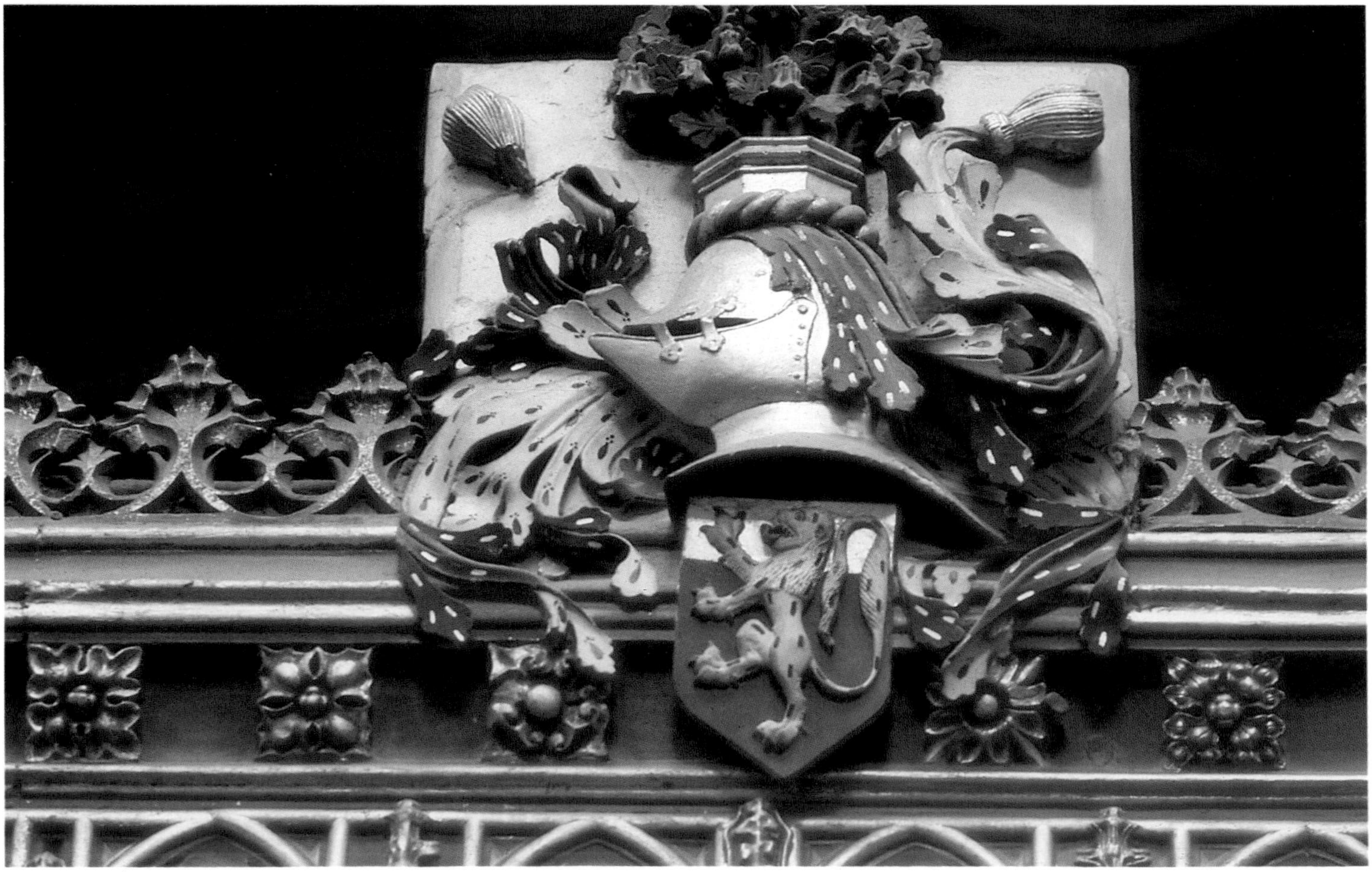

*The arms attributed to the devil.*

*Two breeds of hound – the greyhound and the talbot – are traditionally used in Heraldry.*

is always shown with powerful tusks and a crest of bristling hair down his back, usually of a different colour. He is usually shown trotting, unless he is a supporter, when he stands on his back legs. He has often been used as a badge. A white boar was the badge of Richard III of England.

**BROCK OR BADGER** He is occasionally found in all roles. He has also been called a 'grey' and is used as a charge by the de Grise family.

**BUCK (FALLOW DEER)** He is distinguished from the stag by his wide, bladed antlers.

**BULL** He is frequently encountered, though usually only the head, with a ring in the nose, is shown. Continental Heraldry makes frequent use of the long, curved horns of the wild bull or auroch, especially on crests, in pairs with pendant feathers.

**DEER** Species of deer and antelope from the New World are gradually being introduced. Deer have a terminology of their own: when *passant* they are called 'trippant'; when *statant guardant*, described as 'at gaze'; when *couchant*, 'lodged'; when running, 'in chase' or 'at speed'; and when *salient*, 'springing'. Antlers (horns) have their own terms as well; they are called 'attires', and the points 'tines'.

**ERMINE** A white stoat usually shown as a fur, he is sometimes found as an animal in his own right.

**FOX** The epitome of slyness and cunning, he is occasionally found.

**FROG** The emblem of the devil, he is still today associated with witchcraft.

**GOAT** He is always shown in typical billy-goat

form, with a rough coat, curved horns and beard. Specific types of goat are also used.

**HEDGEHOG** Also called an urchin and, in French, an 'herrison', he is borne by the family of Harris.

**HORSE** A symbol of speed and bravery, the horse was the emblem of the Saxon kings of England.

He is rarely found, though the head appears as a crest and a charge. He is far more common, of course, in the form of the unicorn.

**HOUND** Though modern breeds of dog are being introduced into Heraldry, traditionally only two breeds were used: the greyhound, as an emblem for a swift messenger, and the talbot, an ancient hunting dog somewhere between a hound and a Great Dane, as an emblem of faithfulness.

**LAMB** He is frequently used as an emblem of Christ.

**RABBIT** He is also known as a 'coney'.

**RAM** He is sometimes found on arms, though not commonly.

**SQUIRREL** He is usually shown red in colour, siting on his haunches with a nut.

**STAG** He is shown as the red deer and is also called hart or royal when of a mature age with twelve points or more on the antlers.

**TIGER** Modern usage shows the striped animal, as we know it, but in ancient times the tyger (as he is spelled in Heraldry) was so far removed from reality as to warrant being included among the monsters.

**WOLF** Though common throughout Europe in medieval times, he is not often found.

*ABOVE LEFT The ferocious boar is frequently seen on badges.*

*MIDDLE LEFT The badger, or brock, is sometimes called a 'grey'.*

*BELOW LEFT The wolf is a rare device in modern Heraldry.*

*ABOVE LEFT The long, curved horns of the wild bull frequently surmount crests.*

*ABOVE Heraldic bears often wear a muzzle, derived from their use as performing animals at medieval fairs.*

## —— THE MONSTERS ——

Monsters in Heraldry are the product partly of mythology and legend, partly of fertile imaginations and partly of ignorance. Heraldic artists composed designs of creatures that they had never seen, based on the tales of travellers who repeated stories heard in far-off lands. However the monsters were created, they offered medieval Heralds perhaps the most colourful devices for Heraldic expression. In the days when the drama and pageant of the tournament and its attendant fairs and entertainments provided the main excitement of the age, the opportunity for display which monsters gave the Heralds was eagerly seized. Someone trying to devise a costume to be worn by his pages as they paraded his shield around the arena had a vast field to exploit once the idea of Heraldic monsters took hold. Think of the costume possibilities for someone trying to express the idea that he was as fierce as a lion, strong as an ox, swift as a horse and cunning as a fox!

The monsters, which, with a few differences, all follow the rules and customs of the animals, fall into several different groups.

*WINGED ANIMALS* These are ordinary animals given wings to lend them a greater mythological significance, like the winged lion of St. Mark, the winged horse, Pegasus, and so on.

*SEA ANIMALS* Many animals, especially the lion and the horse, are turned into sea monsters by giving them fish tails or fins. The sea-dog, for example, has fins instead of feet, a fin along the back and a tail like the beaver's.

*MYTHOLOGICAL MONSTERS* There are numerous mythological monsters, but most of them are variants of the five which follow.

**DRAGON** He is a four-legged monster with thick, scaly skin like armour, a long tail ending with a sting, bat-like wings and a horned head with a forked tongue, prominent teeth and claws. He can be of any colour.

**PHOENIX** He is an eagle, with a tuft on his head, rising from the flames.

**SALAMANDER** He is a lizard, sitting in flames, unhurt.

**UNICORN** A horse with a long single horn on its head, the unicorn is an animal of great beauty and allure, said to have been used as a symbol for Christ because by legend he could be caught only by a virgin who tamed him.

**WYVERN** He is in effect a two-legged dragon. When blazoned properly he is green with a red chest and belly and red underwings.

*ABOVE LEFT AND ABOVE The addition of fish tails and fins turns land animals into Heraldic sea monsters.*

*LEFT The dragon can be of any colour; this is the red dragon of Wales.*

County of Avon

*LEFT A brass plate etched by P G Marden shows sea stags used as supporters by Avon County on its Coat of Arms.*

*ABOVE The Achievement of Arms of Cynon Valley Borough shown here was moulded in resin.*

*A detail from the Rous Roll, depicting the arms of*
*Richard III of England and his wife Anne Neville,*
*showing the boar badge used by him and by his son.*

# More About Monsters Composed of Human Beings

The heraldic imagination has conjured up a variety of monsters, part human, part creature and these have been displayed on arms, as supporters and as crests. Sometimes as badges.

MANDRAKE The mandrake is in fact a plant with a knobbly root, which is said to resemble the human figure. It is said to let out such a shriek when pulled out of the ground that it makes all those who hear it deaf. It is attributed with considerable medical properties and though rarely used in heraldry in England, it is more common on the continent.

MERMAID Fabulous creatures of the deep, that might lure those foolhardy enough to venture upon the seas to a watery grave by their desirable beauty, have been a part of the legends of man ever since the first sailor settled in front of the evening fire and told with misty eye the perils of his adventures. It used to be the belief that every creature on the land had its counterpart in the sea and so sea dogs, sea lions, sea horses, sea wolves and sea men and women were perfectly acceptable creatures. A mermaid is always depicted as a beautiful woman with a fish tail from the naval downwards. She is usually shown looking into a mirror and combing her hair, though she occasionally holds other items.

MELUSIN There is a variant of the mermaid, the Melusin, who is depicted with two tails, which she holds in each hand. She is more common in continental heraldry. She is sometimes said to have snake's tails, but is usually depicted with fish's.

MERMAN The merman appears rarely and, as he is a frightening creature, is not often used. He has no special attributes and can be shown holding anything or nothing, He can be dressed in armour.

TRITON When the merman holds a trident and has a conch shell, through which he can blow up a storm, he becomes a Triton.

HARPY The harpy is definitely a creature not to be lightly displayed. They have been described as hags whose duty it was to snatch away the souls of the dead and carry them away to the gods. They were reputed to be very fierce and would slay any man that they met but were filled thereafter with remorse. They are depicted in a variety of ways. An eagle with a man's face. The same with a woman's face. In the arms of the City of Nuremberg, a harpy is depicted with a crowned woman's face and torso and eagle's legs, tail and wings.

SAGITTARY This creature, like the centaur, is half man, half creature; in this case it is half lion. It displays the torso of a man holding a bow and arrow and the body and four legs of a lion.

EGYPTIAN SPHINX This creature is usually depicted couchant (that is lying down) with the body of a lion and the head and beard of a man with an Egyptian headdress.

GREEK SPHINX The Greek sphinx is usually shown sejant (sitting upright) and has wings, with the face and bust of a woman.

MANTICORE OR MANTYGER This creature, fairly rare in appearance, has a lion's body and a man's head. He has three rows of voracious teeth and is sometimes shown with tusks, like a boar.

MANDRAKE

MERMAID

MERMAN

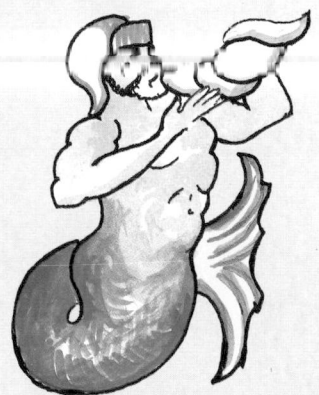

TRITON

SAGITTARY

*The chained porcupine crest of the Countess of Sussex,*
*on her tomb in Westminster Abbey.*

## MONSTERS COMPOSED OF MORE THAN ONE ANIMAL

**BONICON** A bull/horse with curled horns, he is useless for attack, but breaks wind with such effect as to devastate several acres behind him.

**COCKATRICE OR BASILISK** He is a wyvern with a cockerel's head.

**ENFIELD** He has a fox's head, a wolf's body, tail and backlegs and an eagle's front legs.

**GRIFFIN OR GRYPHON** He has the head, breast, wings and foreclaws of an eagle and the body, tail and hind legs of a lion. He also has pointed ear tufts. The griffin is a very strong monster and should always be drawn as such, combining the characteristics of the eagle, king of the birds, with those of the lion, king of the beasts. A griffin *rampant* is said to be 'segreant'. Male griffins have a bunch of long spikes instead of wings and spikes sticking out of other parts of the body.

**HERALDIC ANTELOPE** He has a lion's body and tail, a dragon's head with long serrated horns, and the legs and hooves of a deer.

**HERALDIC TYGER** He resembles a lion in form, but with a longer snout, turned-down horn on the end, and tusks in the lower jaw. He is usually coloured bright red. He is very swift and the only thing to do if you wish to steal his cubs is to throw down a mirror, thereby delaying the tyger long enough for you to get away. For this reason he is often shown looking back into a hand mirror on the ground.

**OPINICUS** He is the same as a griffin, but with four lion's legs.

**OUNCE** This is a mythical beast resembling the leopard. In Heraldry he is sometimes shown as a black panther.

**PANTHER** He resembles the real animal in form, but is usually coloured white and covered with multi-coloured spots. He is always shown as incensed, that is, with flames issuing from his ears and mouth. Some people argue that these are in fact the sweet breath which excites other animals, but puts the fear of death into dragons, on whom the panther preys.

**YALE** He has the body and legs of a goat, a long nose and tusks like those of a boar. He has two curving horns, which swivel in any direction to fend off attack. One horn is usually shown with pointing forward, the other backwards.

## MONSTERS COMPOSED OF HUMAN BEINGS

**CENTAUR** He has the body and legs of a horse joined to the torso of a man.

**HARPY** This is usually shown as an eagle with a woman's head and breasts, though sometimes with only the head. Some versions have a woman's torso and head with an eagle's wings and legs.

**MANDRAKE** This is the head of a man with a poisonous root attached to it.

**MELUSIN** This is a mermaid with two tails.

**MERMAID** This is the top half a nude woman and the bottom half a fish tail. She is usually shown looking into a mirror, combing her hair.

**MERMAN** This is a male mermaid.

**SAGITTARY** He has the body and limbs of a lion joined to the torso, arms and head of a man.

**SPHINX** This is not a very common charge in Heraldry. It takes two forms: the Greek sphinx is shown winged with the face and bust of a woman and the body of a lion; the Egyptian sphinx has the face of a man in the head-dress of Pharoah and the body of a lion and is always shown couchant.

**TRITON** This is a merman holding a trident and blowing into a shell trumpet. He is occasionally shown in armour, as on the arms of the Worshipful Company of Fishmongers in London.

*The griffin is always drawn as a powerful, fierce monster and as either male or female (see page 44 ).*

*The centaur has the torso of a man and the body and legs of a horse.*

*The yale has a goat's body and legs, and two horns, one usually shown facing backwards, the other forwards, as here.*

FAR LEFT *The lamb is frequently used as a symbol of Christ.*

LEFT *The ounce, a mythical beast resembling a leopard, appears in Heraldry often as a black panther, as here.*

# Examples of Birds in Heraldry

**OWL**

Appears often as a crest and a charge, as a symbol of wisdom and learning.

**SWAN**

Frequently found. In England it is a royal bird and is used as charge, supporter and badge. A ' swan argent ducaly gorged (with a duke's crown round its neck) and chained or ', is the badge of the Duke of Buckingham and has become much associated with the heraldry of Buckinghamshire.

**PEACOCK**

Has long been a symbol of royalty in eastern countries. It appears infrequently and when shown with its tail displayed is known as a 'peacock in its pride'.

**PELICAN**

Usually shown as a female tearing her own breast to feed her young and known as a 'pelican in her piety'.

**MARTLET**

This bird, which frequently appears as a charge is thought to represent the swift. Since the swift never lands, except to nest, it has been used as a sign for a younger son, one who has no land of his own, no place to rest. It is also thought that because it was so common in the Holy Land, it became an emblem of one who had been on a pilgrimage.

**DOVE**

Shown carrying a laurel branch, has become an internationally known emblem of peace and hope. But, it is far more likely that it will be drawn standing, with a small crest and it may or may not have one wing raised. As such it will be found on the arms of the College of Heralds in England. The Egyptians understood the homing instinct of the bird and used it to carry messages. It could be that this charge alludes to the herald's role in carrying messages for his master, across frontiers, unhindered.

**BITTERN**

Appears as the crest of Barnadiston and is drawn stalking between bullrushes but has a more characteristic pose which it adopts when seeking to remain undiscovered.

**COCK**

Like many other things, the cock appeared in art and symbolism long before heraldry was established as a recognizable art form. In Christian art, it is employed as a sign of the call to repentance. As foretold, St Peter denied Jesus three times before the cock crowed and it appears on top of many Christian churches in the form of a weather vane. In heraldry, because of its pugnacity it is employed by military persons.

**CORMORANT**

An emblem of sea power.

**STORK**

Often shown standing on one leg, holding in its other foot a stone. Drawn thus, it is known as a 'stork in her vigilance'. If she falls asleep she will drop the stone onto her other foot and wake up!

**LAPWING**

Tyrwhitt bears gules, three tyrwhitts (peewits) or.

**MOORCOCK**

You will often see this bird drawn looking like a cockerel, with two stiff tail feathers sticking straight

OWL

SWAN

PEACOCK

PELICAN

MARLETT

DOVE

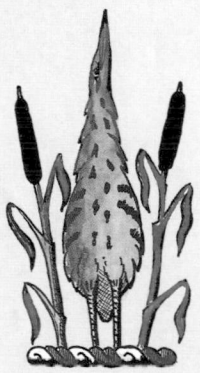

BITTERN
(CREST OF
BARNADISTON)

BITTERN

STORK IN HER
VIGILANCE

out and perhaps one could describe it as a 'heraldic-moorcook'. The moorcook is in fact the Blackcock and perhaps a more realistic rendition, whilst endeavouring to maintain the heraldic postures and ideal, might be more apt. Middlemore bears as a crest a moorcook midst grasses and reeds, proper. And Moore displayed argent three moorcooks sable.

## GROUSE, CAPERCALIE, PHEASANT AND PARTRIDGE

The Worshipful Company of Cooks displays a pheasant as a crest and Partridge displays gules three partridges proper.

## PARROT, EMU, OSTRICH AND OTHER EXOTIC BIRDS

Appear as emblems or supporters for people working overseas. The ostrich has appeared in heraldry since earliest times and, because of his pugnacious nature at certain times of the year and his habit of eating indigestible objects, has been used by fighting men and as an emblem of toughness.

## PENGUIN AND ALBATROSS

Appear for those who have ventured into southern waters, though the albatross has the additional attribute of being applicable to someone who has wandered.

## GUILLIMOT AND DUCKS OF DIFFERENT KINDS

Appear as supporters.

## HERON

Appear, allusive to fishing rights and are occasionally depicted with objects in their beak.

## CHOUGH

This small black bird, similar in size and conformation to our well-know jackdaw, but being black all over with red beak and legs, is associated particularly in England with Cornwall where it can be found.

## SMALL BIRDS

As well as the great birds some of the little birds appear as well. Kay has a goldfinch in their crest and Clarke has a Lark.

## CROW

Crows, known as corbies are displayed by a family of that name.

## EAGLE

There are many examples of eagles preying on other creatures and examples of eagles legs and heads used as charges. In German heraldry, the displayed eagles wing appears often in pairs as a crest.

## FALCONRY

This was a very important sport and method of obtaining food in the Middle Ages, and Greenland falcons, Gyrfalcons, peregrines and goshawks were captured and trained to hunt. Falcons often appear in heraldry, and are usually depicted 'jessed and belled'. The falcon wore a small bell on its leg fastened with thin leather jesses, so that the falconer could find it if it alighted in a wood. Falcon bells appear as charges, as do the little hat or hood that was put on them to keep them sitting quietly on the falconer's hand. The falconer could bring a falcon back to his hand by whirling a lure (composed of two bird wings and a piece of meat) around his head. Depictions of these lures appear as charges. Wingfield bore argent on a bend gules three lures argent. Happily this ancient sport is enjoying a considerable revival today and many people have a chance to see these majestic birds flying in demonstrations. This most ancient of sports has found a new lease of life with our most modern of machines, the jet aircraft. Damage to highly expensive jet engines is being caused by birds being sucked in at take off and landing. The potential for catastrophe is enormous and so airfields are regularly using falconers to keep flocks of gulls, lapwings, starlings and pigeons away from airfields.

HERALDIC MOORCOCK

MOORCOCK

EAGLE'S LEG

EAGLE'S HEAD
(ERASED)

FALCON

LURE

*Crests commonly feature ostrich feathers, as does the famous badge of the Prince of Wales.*

ABOVE RIGHT *These arms show the use of a woodwose as a supporter on the right; human monsters are usually employed as supporters in this way, rather than as charges. An exception is the shield of the Wood family, which shows three wood-woses in fesse.*

BIRD POSTURES

ADDORSED

DISPLAYED

DOUBLE-HEADED

INVERTED

RISING

SOARING

OPPOSITE *This stained-glass window, made by Jane Gray, shows the arms of the Worshipful Company of Launderers.*

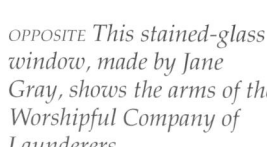

## BIRDS IN HERALDRY

There are a number of terms that apply to all birds in Heraldry.

*ADDORSED* With the wings back-to-back.

*ARMED* Of the colour of the claws.

*BEAKED* Of the colour of the beak, as in a 'swan argent beaked gules'.

*BELLED* Of a falcon, with the falconer's bell attached.

*CLOSE* Standing on the ground with wings closed.

*CROWNED* With a crown on its head of the specified colour.

*DISPLAYED* Of a bird placed on the shield affrontly, with both wings and the legs and tail spread out and head turned to the dexter (with two heads, then each looking outwards).

*DOUBLE-HEADED* With two heads and neck, joined at the shoulders.

*ELEVATED* With wing tips pointing upwards.

*GORGED* With a collar encircling the neck or gorge.

*INVERTED* With the wing tips turned down.

*JESSED* Of a falcon, with the bell tied on to the leg with a jess.

*MEMBERED* Of the colour of the legs.

*RISING* Of the bird standing on the ground with wings raised.

*SOARING* Flying like an eagle or lark.

*VOLANT* Flying across the shield.

*VULNING* Wounding.

## FISHES & SHELLS, INSECTS & REPTILES

Practically every known creature has been employed in the services of Heraldry and these last groups are as important as the more impressive beasts of the field.

### ———— THE FISHES ————

The dolphin must be the commonest of fish, but all kinds are employed, in all the postures so far described for other beings. Fish also have some terms of their own.

*EMBOWED* Formed in a graceful curve, usually as of a dolphin.

*NAIANT* Swimming across the shield, heads to the dexter.

*HAURIENT* Swimming up to the top of the shield.

*URIANT* Swimming down to the bottom of the shield.

Fish are frequently used in arms to allude to the name of the bearer and they sometimes appear of no specified type. They can be used as charges and crests. The crest of the Solomon Islands, for example, has an alligator and a shark haurient as supporters and that of the Bahamas bears a swordfish and a flamingo.

## TERMS APPLIED TO FISH

EMBOWED

NAIANT

HAURIENT    URIANT

DEMI-LUCE

*Illustrated here are the common postures of Heraldic fish.*

ESCALLOP

WHELK

*The escallop is a more common shell in Heraldry than the whelk*

RIGHT *The tomb of Lord Hunsdon in the St John the Baptist Chapel of Westminster Abbey; among his other armorial cognizances is his crest, a swan wings addorsed and elevated proper.*

###### —— THE SHELLS ——

The escallop is the most commonly used shell-fish, and frequently denotes that the bearer has been on a pilgrimage or is a pilgrim in the metaphorical sense of the word. Three escallop shells on a shield cannot be taken to mean that the bearer has been on three pilgrimages. Whelk shells also appear.

###### —— THE INSECTS ——

The bee as a symbol of industry is popularly used, as is the spider. Other insects only rarely appear.

###### —— THE REPTILES ——

Lizards and snakes appear, but are not very common. Other reptiles are rare, though there are modern examples of crocodiles.

*NOWED* Knotted, as applying, for example, to a snake or lizard tail.

*COILED* With the head erect and in a posture ready to strike.

*GLISSANT* Gliding.

## HUMAN AND CELESTIAL BEINGS

Human and celestial beings occur frequently in Heraldry and all the appropriate terms applied to beasts and birds apply to them as well.

###### —— CELESTIAL BEINGS ——

It is more common to find allusion to heavenly people by symbol than by direct representation. Examples do exist of Christ on the Cross, but very rarely, since it was felt to be improper to reduce so sacred a subject to Heraldry. Though Inverness in Scotland bears 'gules upon a cross the figure of Our Lord crucified proper', most of the very few representations of Christ, of his mother or of the saints are found on the arms of ecclesiastical establishments. Some European towns display saints, but this is not a common practice. Angels occasionally appear as supporters, both officially and unofficially, but again the practice is rare. In modern Heraldry an angel is usually represented as a female figure, vested in a long robe, with wings. Historically angels belonged to a variety of different orders, each portrayed differently. Angel supporters are frequently used to display shields, as a decorative feature, when shown in churches.

**THE ARCHANGELS** Archangels were definitely felt to be gentlemen in the medieval imagination and arms were attributed to them. The only one of heraldic significance is St. Michael. He is usually depicted in armour, carrying out the fight against the Devil, who is represented by a green dragon. His arms were a red cross on a white field. He was evidently the model for the mythical St. George, who is now the patron saint of chivalry and of England.

**CHERUB** He is shown as the face of a boy, above a pair of wings.

**SERAPHIM** He is shown as a man's face, with six wings, but only rarely.

**CUPID** A mythical rather than celestial being. The figure of Cupid does appear and is shown as a young boy, with wings and a bow and arrow. It is important not to confuse Cupid and Cherubs with the more familiar 'puti' so beloved of baroque art and sculpture which have no symbolism, but are used for purely artistic effect.

**MERCURY** Appears as a crest and charge and so do winged hands and feet. The Caducus, his serpent entwined staff, is also used as a charge.

**APOLLO** Appears as the main charge of the arms of the Worshipful Company of Apothecaries.

Apart from their use as supporters, representations of the whole human figure belong more to religious art and mythology than to heraldry though there are quite a number of instances of human monsters. These imaginary combinations of human and creature that so fire the imagination are discussed further on, in the section about monsters.

###### —— HUMAN BEINGS ——

The whole human figure is often used as a supporter in all kinds of costume and styles, but it is comparatively rare to find it as a charge, for which purpose it is more common to find hands, heads, legs and hearts, either vested or armoured, in a large variety of ways. Parts of the human body can be erased or couped in the same way as parts of animal bodies.

**HEAD** – *profile* the head is placed facing dexter. It can be cut off at the neck or across the shoulders and the type – a maiden, a Saxon, a Saracen, a Turk and so on – should be specified in the blazon. It can wear any kind of crown or wreath.

**DEMI-FIGURE** This is a very common crest, and may be armoured (in armour), habited (vested) or vested (dressed in). It is often carrying an object and is sometimes seen wearing a helm and the crest itself repeated in little.

**ARMS** are often found as charges and crests. As crests they are usually found holding something in the hand. The blazon will sometimes say which arm it is. A 'cubit arm' is one arm cut off cleanly below the elbow. 'Embowed' means 'bent at the shoulder', 'Vambraced' means 'in armour' and 'Vested and cuffed' means 'within a sleeve with a different coloured cuff'.

**HANDS** Hands are commonly used as a charge. The blazon will always say if right or left. 'Apaumy' means 'open, showing the palm' and 'Closed' means 'clenched or grasping an object'.

**LEGS** Legs are found used in the same way. Whether they are cut off at, above or below the knee will be stated in the blazon. Arms and legs can be placed either vertically ('palewise') erect or horizontally ('fesswise').

**WOODWOSE** These are wild men and women of the woods, usually depicted as hairy all over and wearing a few leaves around the loins.

*ABOVE An illustration from Froizart's Chronicles, a 14th century manuscript; the English army campaign in France under the banner of St George.*

*OPPOSITE FAR RIGHT Church funeral hatchments; the hatchment on the right shows 'or three piles piercing a human heart gules' for Hart Logan.*

essire Jehan de
auec ceulx qui

bloys fut pris des anglois.

FAR LEFT The arm is described as 'vambraced' (in armour), holding a battle-axe.

LEFT This illustration shows a cubit arm (cut off cleanly below the elbow); it is described as vested because of the sleeve; vested and cuffed, in a blazon, means that the cuff is of a different colour from the sleeve.

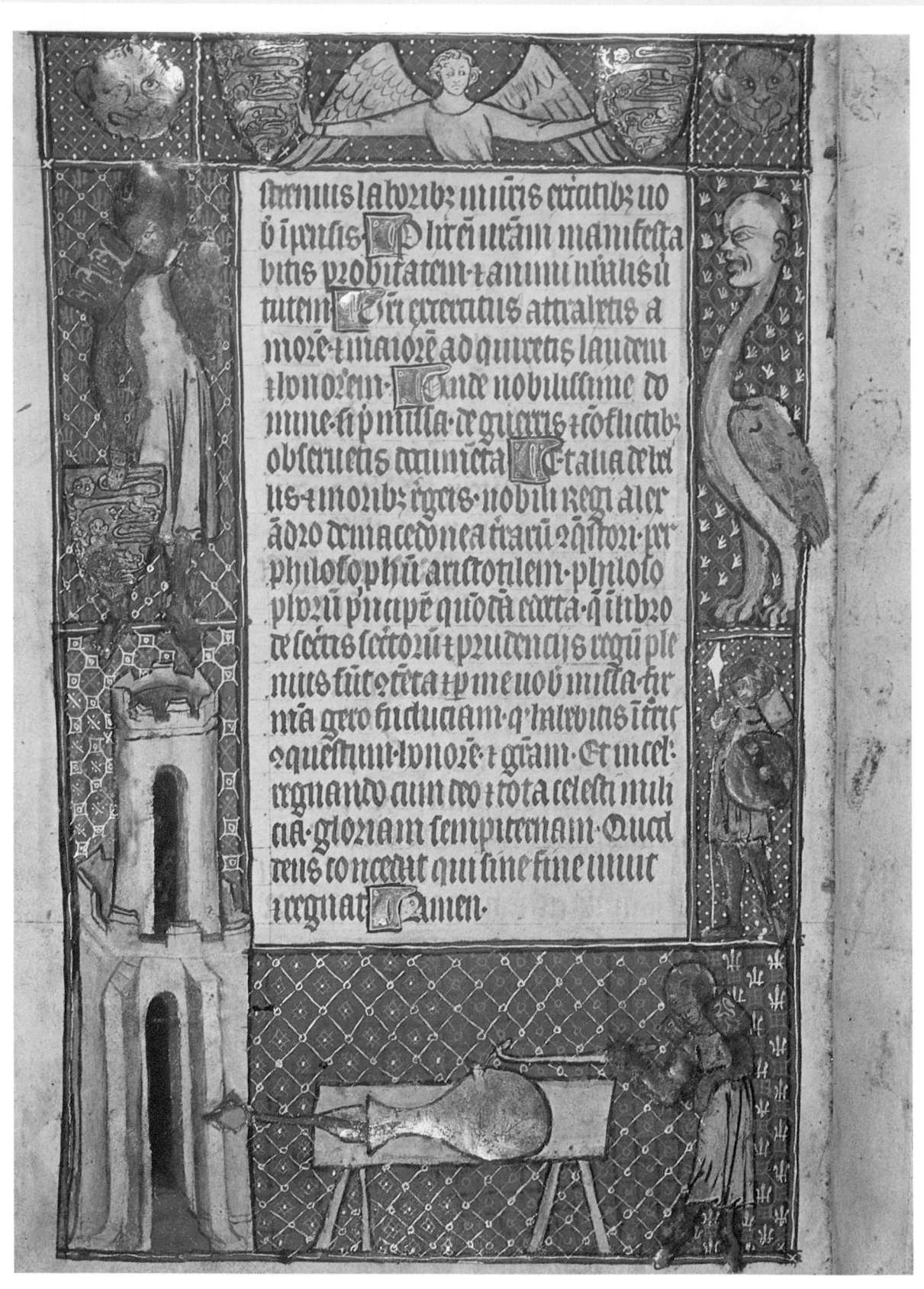

*An illuminated canon (1326) from Christchurch,
Oxford, showing an angel bearing the Royal arms of
England.*

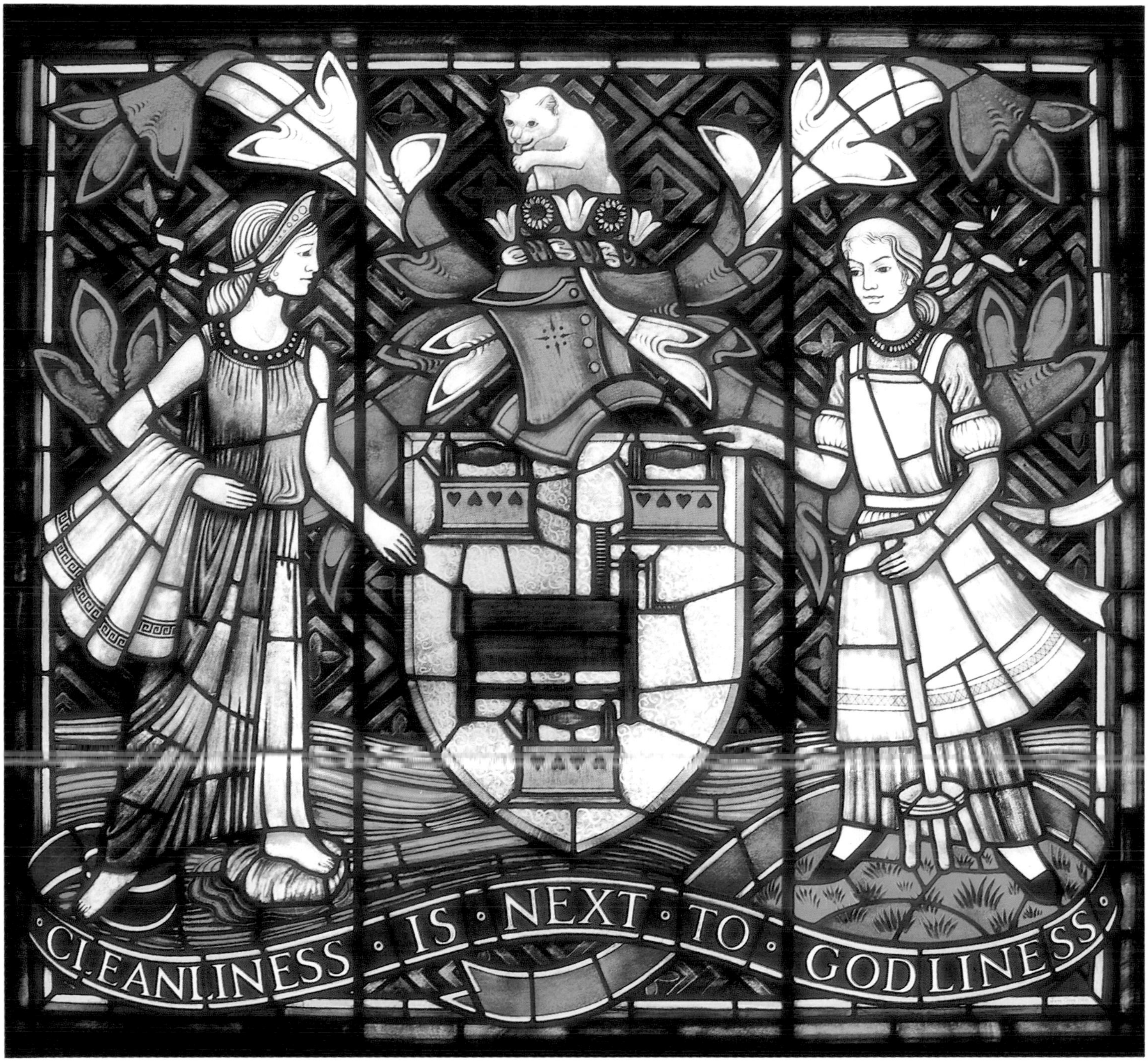

CLEANLINESS · IS · NEXT · TO · GODLINESS

FAR LEFT *Illustrated here are the armorial bearings of the Worshipful Company of Vintners.*

CENTRE LEFT *The arms of the United States display the eagle as a single supporter.*

NEAR LEFT *The figure of St Margaret is used as a crest for the arms of the Borough of Lowestoft.*

# CHAPTER SEVEN

# Plants and Inanimate Objects

*The Heraldic rose is nearly always shown in a stylized form. The Tudor Rose of England (right) amalgamates the red rose of the House of Lancaster and the white rose of the House of York.*

ℒIKE the beasts and birds, all kinds of plants, flowers, leaves and trees appear in general use.

## THE FLOWERS

*LILY* The queen of the plants is depicted either as the stylized fleur de lis, which can be in a variety of different forms, or as the natural flower.

*ROSE* The rose, if you like, is the king of the flowers. It is nearly always shown in a stylized form, the Heraldic rose. 'Slipped and leaved proper', which applies to other flowers as well as the rose, means that the outer green sepals and the leaves are shown on a short length of green stalk. 'Seeded' refers to the colours of the centre.

*THISTLE* This is usually shown 'slipped and leaved proper' as the national emblem of Scotland. It is very much associated with that country and people who have emigrated from it.

*QUATREFOIL* This is a stylized four-petal flower.

*CINQUEFOIL* This is a stylized five-petal flower.

These last two are sometimes found with the centre pierced with a hole.

*FRAISE (OR FRASE, FRAZE)* This is a white cinquefoil representing the strawberry flower and is used on the Coat of Arms of Fraiser, 'gules three fraises'.

## THE PLANTS

*BROOM OR PLANTA GENESTA* This is a sprig showing the leaves, flowers and pods and is a well-known badge of the Plantagenet kings of England.

*TREFOIL LEAF* This is a well known three-leafleted charge.

*MAPLE LEAF* This appears in Canadian Heraldry. The maple leaf is the official emblem of Canada.

*HOLLY LEAF* This appears in Scottish Heraldry as a charge and is held up in a hand in a crest.

*OAK LEAVES* These appear throughout Europe, as do acorns.

*WHEATEARS* These are also quite common throughout most of Europe.

*GARB* This commonly is a sheaf of wheat, but can be of other things.

## THE TREES

Trees of all kinds appear as charges and crests. They are quite often shown growing 'from a mound'. 'Acorned' means of an oak with acorns. 'Fructed' means with fruit as in the Orange Free State in South Africa, and which bears 'or on a mound vert an orange tree fructed proper'. 'Eradicated' means a tree shown up-rooted.

*Many stylized versions of the lily are found in Heraldry.*

*RIGHT Two shields in the stone of Lincoln Cathedral; The Farr shield (LEFT) shows a saltar with four fleur de lis. The shield of Weller (RIGHT) displays three roses.*

*OPPOSITE LEFT The armorial bearings of the Hambledon District Council were moulded in resin by de Havilland & Howell.*

*OPPOSITE FAR RIGHT The arms of Astley of Norfolk on Norwich Cathedral, showing a cinquefoil ermine pierced in the first quarter.*

UNITED IN PROGRESS

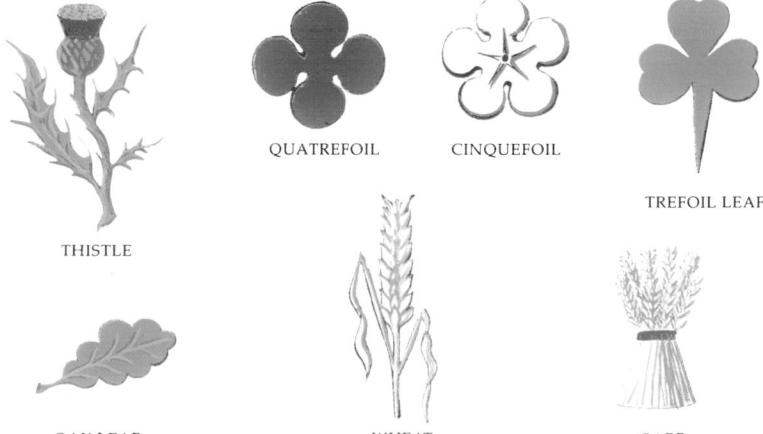

THISTLE

QUATREFOIL

CINQUEFOIL

TREFOIL LEAF

OAK LEAF

WHEAT

GARB

# Flowers in Heraldry

The use of flowers and plants in heraldry is so widespread that this makes a special and fascinating study of its own, full of inspiring material borrowed from the symbolism and culture of other earlier traditions and ideals. Herein lies one of the strengths and charms of heraldry and a possible clue as to why the art has endured and indeed flourished for so long after its actual usage has passed. Heraldry is able to assimilate and adapt symbolism from all walks of life and can use and incorporate ideas that reflect all aspects of that life, past, present and in the future. There is no limit to what might be incorporated into heraldic symbolism and this is to the enduring benefit of the art.

The plants and flowers found so abundantly in creation are equally abundantly used in heraldry, in their magnificent and plentiful variety. But how can it be that these beautiful and completely unbellicose objects should find themselves part of the tools of an art from that derived its necessity from warfare?

It is true that heraldry as we know it today has evolved over the centuries and that many of the devices employed have come from other and earlier civilizations and artistic concepts. This evolution was considerably boosted by the efforts of the early Christian knights to rid the Holy Land of the invading Turks and by the fact that warfare had developed at the same time to the stage when the knights were so encased in chain mail and armour that it was impossible to tell who was who. The need for a plainly visible scheme of personal identification was very real.

If the basic need was a military one, why then choose a rose, that emblem of love? It would hardly strike terror into the heart of the foe. Far better to choose a lion to show how fierce you were or a severed head to show what happened to your adversaries. There must have been some reason why these beautiful emblems, on the face of it more suited to decorate a ladies boudoir than a shield of war, were chosen. I would like to suggest that reason was the Christian religion.

If we are to explore that reason, we must first look more deeply into the ethos of Medieval society. Without question the great dominating factor of the age, the pendulum of the life of the time, the mainspring of motivation, was Christianity and the Christian way of life. Look at the wonderful ecclesiastical buildings that remain, erected in the 12th, 13th, 14th and 15th Centuries all over Europe. Relatively few domestic buildings of that age survive. It was obviously more important for a successful person to endow a magnificent and enduring church in the hope that the pious act might help his immortal soul, than to provide for his bodily comfort whilst still living. The fantastic works of art that remain to us of those days are nearly all of a religious nature. People gave their lives for and to the Christian ideal, as is witnessed by the Crusades, the orders of Chivalry and the great monastic institutions, some of which remain to this day.

People hoped that they would go to the Holy Land before they died, and some of the earlier orders of knights were made up of people, often younger sons, without much hope of any inheritance from home, who gave up everything to assist and defend these

pilgrims on their journey. As the threat to the Holy places from the invasions of the Turks increased, Orders of Knights were established to defend them as best they could and many lost their lives in the conflicts that followed.

When the Turks finally over-ran Jerusalem and the Christians were driven out, the Popes of that time called the Crusades. They offered, by the power that had been handed down to them from the Saviour himself though the successors of St Peter, plenary indulgences, complete remission and forgiveness of all sin, a free pass straight into Heaven to any who died attempting to liberate the Holy Lands, so that Christian pilgrims might visit them again. Parties of knights went from all over Europe, hoping that they might succeed, but assured that if they failed they would achieve their life's ambition and be able to stand in the presence of God. The Crusades drew knights from all over Europe who went in groups, selecting their own personal emblems, but all displaying the cross in one of its many forms on their banners, and on the shoulders of their cloaks. Of course there were many, as in any ideological conflict, who went along for the adventure, for the fight or for what they could earn or grab for themselves, but I would like to suggest that even amongst those there were some who hedged their bets and selected religious-type emblems, just in case!

It would be quite wrong to suggest that every emblem in heraldry had a religious significance and most, quite plainly, have none at all. Some express sovereign prowess or domination. Some show bellicose intent, some are allusive to the arms of an overlord or have some connection to the name of the bearer. Some allude to occupation or office, but some, just a few, are a puzzle and this certainly applies to flowers and flower-like objects. Since, on the surface, flowers seem unsuitable for heraldry (most unlikely to strike terror into the heart of an enemy) there must be some higher reason for why they are so commonly used. I would like to advance the theory that they are religious emblems, perfectly understood by people of the time and that they were chosen to invoke divine protection for the bearer. I would like to submit that medieval Christianity had a far greater effect on people than has been hitherto allowed, admitted, or even considered today.

The religious ethos of our times have been largely shaped by events that took place in the 16th century. A great wave of reforming protest swept through Europe and much that was important and vital before that time was deliberately dismantled and destroyed. Through the gradual secularization of the years this has been all but forgotten. There is no doubt that the Church was in need of reformation and that it had assumed a role and temporal powers that were completely at odds with its foundation. Popes and bishops had set themselves up as kings and princes and they held power over all the kings of western Europe. They held tenure over land in every kingdom and had accrued temporal wealth that ignored the tenants of the Saviour. They forgot that 'He had come to serve, not to rule' and that His Kingdom was not of this world, but of the next. They forgot that when He sent His apostles out, He told them to take nothing and that theirs was the care of souls. They knew the path to Heaven and it was their role to show it to others.

So much of the money and land donated by the wealthy in the hope of expiation of their temporal wrongs and the salvation of their immortal souls, was used to establish a temporal state that was powerful enough to dominate the whole of western Europe. Unfortunately, as is often the case, when the Reformation came it swept aside the good, the bad and the ugly alike. The bad, the rotten apples in the barrel, caused the good to be rejected with the dross and much of what had gone before: people's faiths, beliefs and ideals, were swept aside by men who, however noble their intent, had deliberately cut themselves off from the spiritual guidance of the Saviour that had been handed down in succession through the centuries.

From that time on the Christian ethos has declined in western Europe and has been gradually replaced by religions that derive their authority from their human founders and not from the Son of God and so do not have the spiritual guidance that is descended in His Universal Church. Unfortunately, much of the symbolism and ecclesiastical art and decoration was destroyed at the same time and we, who live in a world of declining religious belief where the ethos of our age is based on the search for leisure, pleasure, personal wealth and gratification, where self comes before commitment to the common good, find the ideals of religious symbolism forgotten and derided.

## TREFOIL

St Patrick used the three lobes of the plant that made up each leaf to demonstrate to the people of Ireland the doctrine of the Holy Trinity. This plant has become therefore an emblem of the Holy Trinity, or indeed of any situation that is, or has been, composed of three parts. St Patrick later became the patron Saint of Ireland and the shamrock has become the national emblem. It is often used to allude to things and people Irish.

## QUATREFOIL

There are many examples of quatrefoils in heraldry and it is usually described as a flower of four petals. The most conspicuous flower of four petals is the poppy and there is no doubt that this could have been the model for this device. I gently submit, however, that this, when brandished at an enemy, bent on death and mayhem, is hardly likely to send him running in terror. It is more likely to evoke his derision and worse still, if in telling of it afterwards, he decides that it was supposed to represent a pansy. It has also been described as a cross made of leaves and it would seem that this might be nearer the truth. There are many different examples of crosses used in heraldry and this just may be another. It may also represent the sign of the cross, made by the user, expressing that what he is about to do is done to the greater glory of God and invoking Divine protection and guidance. The trefoil and quatrefoil shapes are often to be seen in the decorative treatment of churches, especially in the stonework in windows and the woodwork of beams, screens and pews. It could be just pure coincidence that these elegant shapes, so suited to occupy the spaces provided by the design of such things, have been used. It could be that these devices are so sympathetic to use in design that they are among that group of natural items which have emerged from the mists of time as being amongst the most perfect of decorations. It could also be that the designers of the churches were taking every chance that they could of reminding the observer of some of the basic tenants of the Christian faith. How much more we would know if the painted decorations of our churches had been preserved and they had not been covered over in purifying white by those who, in seeking to return to a simpler, more uncluttered religion, destroyed, removed or just threw them away.

## CINQUEFOIL

This is often described as a stylized, five leafed or petalled flower and there are many flowers that it could be said to represent. Indeed, in some cases we know that the cinquefoil is intended to represent a specific flower. Fraser bears gules three fraises (white cinquefoils to represent strawberry flowers). Lord Roseberry bears vert three primroses within a double tressure, flory, counter flory.

It is possible that it is simply corruption, through bad drawing, of the rose, but there are very many instances of its use and this is unlikely to be the case. If then it is to be treated as a separate item, what is it supposed to represent? The plain description is not satisfying enough. How did it find its way into heraldic art and what was it supposed to represent? Considering all that has been said, it is not impossible to consider this emblem especially when pierced, as representing the wounds of Christ.

## OCTOFOIL

There are no six or seven leafed foils and so the existence of this charge must evoke some attention. What is the significance of eight? If there is any credence in the idea of these emblems being based in Christian symbolism, it does not take long to discover that the octofoil must be the representation of the Beatitudes, those great virtues explained by Jesus in what has now become known as the Sermon on the Mount:

> *Blessed be the poor in spirit, for theirs is the Kingdom of Heaven.*
>
> *Blessed are the meek, for they shall possess the land.*
>
> *Blessed are they that mourn, for they shall be comforted.*
>
> *Blessed are they that are hungry and thirst for justice, for they shall have their fill.*
>
> *Blessed are the merciful, for they shall find mercy.*
>
> *Blessed are the clean of heart, for they shall see God.*
>
> *Blessed are the peacemakers for they shall be called the children of God.*
>
> *Blessed are they that suffer persecution for justice's sake for theirs is the Kingdom of Heaven.*

A single symbol that expresses all the ideals and aspirations of those who were prepared to dedicate their lives in helping others in the service of God.

## HERALDIC ROSE

The heraldic rose is drawn to look like the wild rose of the hedgerows and is shown with a single row of petals and with yellow seed heads in the centre. Indeed it has been described by some as the exact representation of the hedgerow flower. In England we think of the rose in patriotic terms – the English Rose, the Tudor Rose, the National Emblem and so on. But are things as obvious as they might appear? Our well-known and well-loved Tudor Rose came into use sometime after the marriage of Henry VII and England and Elizabeth of York as a symbol of the final unity of these two warring factions that had been at each other's throats for nigh on 100 years. If we are to believe the Shakespearean version of the story, each party plucked a rose from a bush and declared it his emblem and the emblem of those who supported him and his House. These roses remained the emblems of the two factions until the strife that followed ended. The House of Lancaster sported a red rose and that of York, white. Display of a red or white rose indicated support for one party or the other. However, the rose was in use as a heraldic charge long before the events of the Wars of the Roses, took place. We need therefore to seek some earlier explanation as to why this object was chosen as an emblem that might serve its wearer in battle. Some research into Christian symbolism will produce a possible answer. An answer that we would all know, understand and accept, had it not been for the Reformation and consequent happenings in this country. The rose was an especial symbol of the Virgin Mary. Such has been the secularization of Christianity in this country and the erosion of faith in the face of rationalism that devotion to her has been relegated almost to the level of a superstition. People forget, or do not know that there was a time when this country was proud to call itself 'the Dowry of Mary'.

A devotion to the Blessed Mother of God grew in England to a level that was unique in the Western World. How this developed is not certain, but it almost certainly evolved from the appearance of the Blessed Virgin to Lady Richolds at Walsingham in the reign of Edward the Confessor. The Virgin Mary,

ARMORIAL BEARINGS OF THE WORSHIPFUL COMPANY OF COOKS

in a vision to that Lady, asked her to build a copy of the house in Nazareth. She assured her that all who visited there to honour the fact that an angel of the Lord appeared to a virgin maiden to tell her that she was chosen to be the mother of the Son of God, would have their prayers answered. The shrine was built in 1061 and in the centuries that followed it became the most important pilgrimage place in the Christian world, next to Jerusalem. The devotion to Our Lady spread all over England, as is witnessed by the number of other shrines that were built and the number of churches that were dedicated to her patronage. This devotion continued in the country until 1538 when the King, instead of nationalizing what would have been a good source of revenue, ordered the destruction of the shrine at Walsingham. This set in train a series of events that ensured that devotion to Our Lady was removed from the national religion. Happily we now live in more enlightened times and people are beginning to realize that the role of Mary is not to reproach or condemn those who take their own way, but help them along the sometimes difficult and precipitous path that leads through her Son, to the Father.

The great prayer to the Mother of God is called the Rosary. This contemplative prayer consists of five parts, each part symbolized by one of the five petals of the rose from which it takes its name. Each one of the petals also stands for one of the five letters MARIA. The string of beads upon which this devotion is counted is also called a rosary.

The saying of the rosary is a meditation upon the life of Our Lady and a supplication for her intercession through her Son, to the Father, for one's earthly difficulties. Each of the five parts of this prayer consider a different episode in Our Lady's life. These episodes, or Mysteries, as they have become called, are represented by different coloured roses: the Glorious Mysteries by a yellow rose; the Joyful Mysteries by a white rose; and the Sorrowful Mysteries by a red rose.

Mary has a unique and much misunderstood place in the mediation between man and God which is the reason for the great devotion to her. It seems natural then for a medieval knight, about to embark on an adventure to free the Holy Lands, to display on his shield a token of supplication to one who could intercede to God on his behalf.

Unfortunately, while this may be the origin of the use of the rose in heraldry, it does not help us with the model for the flower itself.

It seems that medieval gardens were not much different to our own and from such illustrations as are available they seem to consist of small walled enclosures – as much to keep wild animals out as to provide shelter for the plants and occupants. It appears that the flowers and plants illustrated were often of an allegorical nature, telling stories to those who understood, and so cannot be taken as reliable indications of what actually might have grown there. However, they do mostly include rose bushes. The space in such a garden must, of necessity, have been limited and it seems unlikely that much would have been given over to the cultivation of a plant that grew in parks, woods and forests and which was almost immune to the ravages of grazing animals. A search through works on the subject of roses reveal that the single red rose was brought back to this country by Edmund Langley, son of Edward I. He was at that time Duke of Lancaster. Apparently, he brought it back from a punitive expedition to the south of France, where it had become established via returning Crusaders. The religious significance of all this to the medieval mind can be readily seen, as can its choice for the Lancastrian emblem. This red rose can still be found and is known today as *Rosa Gallica*. The white rose, also, is not native to this country. It was apparently introduced to England by the Romans and is still available today, *Rosa Alba*.

LILY

Much has been written about the lily and it has become accepted as the emblem of purity. As such it

has been used as an emblem for Our Lady and for her husband, St Joseph. It is also used as an emblem for St Anthony. In heraldic art it is usually shown as a white, only partly open, flower of three petals with two yellow T-shaped stamens, one either side of the central petal.

## FLEUR DE LYS

There are many theories about the origin of this charge and about what it is supposed to represent. It has been extensively used as an emblem in French heraldry and has been associated with the Royal House. Legend has it that it was given to Clovis, King of France by St Dennis. Others say that his soldiers plucked the flower and wore it in their hats. Others say that his soldiers waved it in the air when wading through a dense reedy marsh so that they could see each other. Most seem to agree that it is an heraldic representation of the yellow marsh 'flag' or iris. Care should be taken not to confuse it with the lily.

## COLUMBINE

Columbine is the floral emblem of the third person of the Holy Trinity, the manifestation of the power of God active in the world, known as the Holy Spirit. The flower of the columbine so represents a group of doves (representations of the Spirit of God) drinking round a bowl that it is easy to see how it got its name and how it was accepted as the flower of the Holy Spirit. In addition, the six points of the flower and the stalk making seven, are the same as the number of the gifts of the Holy Spirit: wisdom, understanding, counsel, fortitude, knowledge, piety and fear of the Lord.

## DAISY

This flower, rarely seen in heraldry, represents humility.

## SUNFLOWER

As well as representing the sun, being gold it also represents money, wealth and good fortune.

## LOTUS

This flower has been brought into heraldry in associ-ation with people who have had connections with the Far East.

## PALM

This represents martyrdom, either in fact or to an ideal,

## LAUREL

These leaves are an ancient emblem of valour and victory.

## OAK LEAVES

These are used to represent valour and steadfastness.

These are just some of the plants and flowers used in heraldry. There is no limit to those that might be used in given circumstances and many are used that have a punning or allusive connotation to the bearer or his name, situation or circumstance.

Whilst it is interesting to speculate about what symbols mean and to muse upon how such unlikely things come to be incorporated into Heraldry, it must must be remembered that times and language change. We can only surmise about what things must have meant to the medieval person in the light of such information as we can glean. It is important to remember that language had a completely different meaning 1,000 years ago and so the employ of our language may give us completely the wrong clues.

Interesting though it may be to try and deduce the possible meaning of such things we are not going to be helped much in our study of heraldry. There may be several different reasons why a particular person has, say, a rose on his shield and in all probability none of them have anything to do with Our Lady. Though in our time, items on shields are chosen with great care and a great deal of research and thought goes into the granting of devices to an aspirant armiger today, the observer can deduce little from looking at the achievement. We can speculate as to why it has been so assembled, but we may well be wrong. It is only if we can see the rationale for the blazon that we can understand what it all means and admire the skill and imagination of the composition.

*ABOVE The portcullis badge of Westminster on a roof boss of Westminster Abbey; this Tudor badge, the Duke of Westminster's badge, is now a common municipal symbol.*

*ABOVE RIGHT Towers are shown in this stone carving of armorial bearings by S & J Winter.*

*ABOVE FAR RIGHT This stained-glass window of the armorial bearings of Sir Peter Tizard was done by Jane Gray.*

## INANIMATE BODIES

This group encompasses all kinds of artefacts, weapons, tools, buildings, ships, every kind of thing imaginable. It is beyond the scope of this book to list everything that might be encountered. The groups are mentioned and attention is drawn to any obscurity or peculiarity in the terms used.

**THE CROSS** By far the most important item is the cross. Because it is the symbol of Christianity and every Christian state took it as its emblem when it set out on the Crusades, there is a bewildering variety of crosses. Some authorities list more than 150. Most of these are very rare; a dozen of the most common varieties are illustrated On page 97.

**THE CELESTIAL BODIES**

*SUN* This is usually shown as the 'sun in splendour', sometimes with a face, sometimes not. 'Sun burst' refers to the representation of a ray of sunlight from behind a cloud.

*MOON* This is shown as a crescent. 'Increscent' refers to a crescent moon facing the dexter; 'Decrescent' refers to a crescent moon facing the sinister; 'In her compliment' refers to the full moon shown with a face to avoid confusion with a plate.

*STARS* A star is always called an estoile and is shown with six or more wavy rays.

*RAINBOW* This appears in the Crest of the Hope family.

*THUNDERBOLT* This appears as a charge, a symbol of wrath, and recently, of electric power.

*CLOUDS* These are usually seen with something issuing from them, sunrays or a hand.

**THE BUILDINGS** A wide range of these are used, but except for the three shown — the tower, the castle, and the bridge — most are rare. These appear as charges, crests and badges. (The portcullis, a defensive gate, is also frequently seen).

CRESCENT MOON

INCRESCENT MOON

DECRESCENT MOON

ESTOILE

SUN BURST

SUN IN SPLENDOUR

TOWER

TOWER TRIPLE-TOWERED

CASTLE

BRIDGE

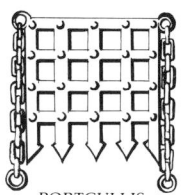

PORTCULLIS

BRIDGE TRIPLE-ARCHED

WINDMILL SAILS

*Illustrated here are the most commonly found buildings in Heraldry.*

SILENTIUM STULTORUM VIRTUS

Professor Sir PETER TIZARD MA DM FRCP

MASTER 1983-1984

**THE WEAPONS** Weapons of all kinds are commonly used throughout Europe and appear as charges, crests and badges and held or brandished by crests and supporters. The most common are the sword, the seax, the battle-axe, the arrow, the arrowhead, the peon, the caltrap, the spear, the tilting spear, the mace and the coronel. The peon is a kind of broad arrowhead and the caltrap is a spiked object which was strewn on the ground to stop horses. The coronel was used to blunt the tip of a tilting spear.

**THE SHIPS** All kinds of ships have been used in Heraldry and the type is usually specified. 'Lymphand', is a galley (trading vessel) in full sail. (Anchors, fish traps, nets, fish spears and tridents have also been used.)

**THE CLOTHING** All kinds of clothing — footwear, hats, armour and gloves — are used as charges. Pilgrim staffs and bags are also seen. A 'Maunch' is a sleeve with pocket pendant.

**THE DOMESTIC ITEMS** Among the most commonly seen domestic items are cups, globes, chess rooks, books, buckles, keys, locks and fetterlocks, mill rinds, clarions, and bougets.

*MILL-RIND* This is the metal bracket which takes the spindle in the centre of a millstone and holds a tie rod on the outside wall of a building.

*CLARION* This is a musical instrument, a kind of trumpet.

*BOUGET* This is a water carrier, consisting of two water buckets made of skin on a yoke.

*FLEAN* This is a kind of surgical instrument, now obsolete.

**THE HERALDIC CROWNS** A variety of crowns are used as charges. They have nothing to do with rank, but serve to denote excellence in a sphere of activity. Note that these are termed crowns, not coronets.

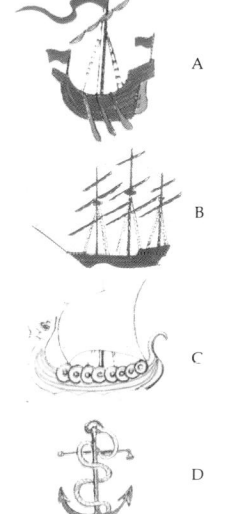

*Ships used in Heraldry include **A** the lymphand **B** the trading vessel, and **C** the Viking ship. Anchors **D** also occur as motifs.*

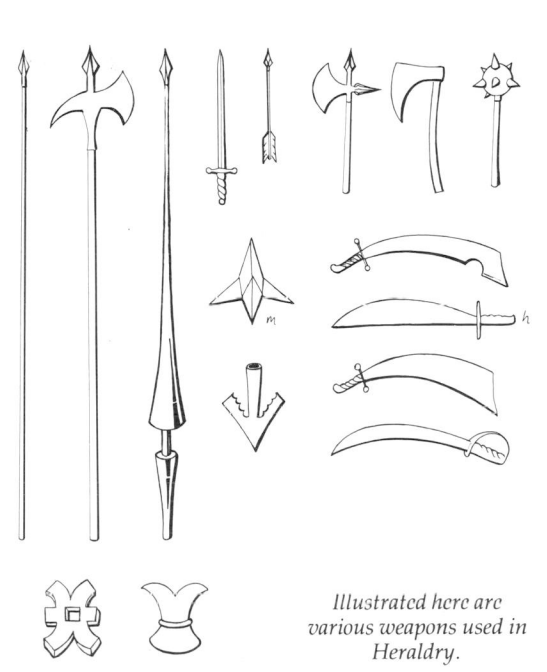

MILL RIND    CHESS ROOK

*Illustrated here are various weapons used in Heraldry.*

ASTRAL

ANCIENT

EASTERN

MURAL

NAVAL

CREST CORONETS

PALISADO

SAXON

VALLARY

*Many different forms of crowns are used as charges.*

# Unusual Charges

Almost every tool and artefact used by man has been incorporated into heraldry, as well as items of clothing of every kind, and some of these may present difficulties to an observer trying to formulate the possible blazon. Indeed, with some modern examples it may be necessary to resort to the original Grant of Arms to ascertain what the charge is supposed to be.

Here are a selection of items, used since ancient times, whose identity may not be readily apparent, but which will from time to time be encountered.

### Mill Rind

This represents the metal plate used to reinforce the centre of a millstone used for grinding flour from wheat. Devices of this kind are also found reinforcing houses. They are seen outside the wall acting as plates for tie-rods that run through the house to prevent the walls from spreading outwards. Nowadays they are often to be seen in the shape of an 'S'. They were sometimes cross-shaped and the crosses moline and recerclé were often used.

### Maunch

This represents the sleeve of a medieval costume. These items were worn over an under garment of some kind and were fastened to the bodice part of the garment by ribbands. It was presumably possible to do a mix and match of different coloured maunches to the main part of the garment and even to each other. These sleeves had pendant from them a long pocket.

### Chess Rook

The chess piece that we know as the pawn. It is drawn in this rather strange way to prevent confusion with the representation of a castle.

### Clarion

This is a kind of wind instrument, not to be confused with the pan pipes, that also appear.

### Bouget

This device should be thought of as a yoke to go over the shoulders, and hung from it two buckets made from animal skin. These were used for carrying water. When armies had to be moved long distances by foot, obviously the provision of water for man and beast was a constant and serious problem.

### Fleam

This charge is used to represent the small instrument that surgeons used to open the vein in the medical practice of blood letting. Apparently it was thought that the symptoms of fever might be relieved through draining blood to reduce the pressure in the patients body.

### Scythe

This long handled instrument was, and still is, used to mow grass and other herbaceous growth and has been included here to make the point that it should not be confused with a fleam.

### Woolsack

In the Middle Ages the wealth of England came from wool. The shorn fleeces were packed and then sewn into large sacks, shown with a tottle at each corner,

so that they could be picked up. They were a symbol of wealth. They should not be confused with a cushion shown with a tassel at each corner, though this is often shown 'lozengy tasseled'.

## GRENADE AND POMEGRANATE

The grenade is shown as a round ball with flames coming out of the top. The pomegranate is usually shown as a round fruit, leafed at the top, but split open and showing the many red seeds inside. It is important not to confuse the two items. The grenade is usually black and the pomegranate green.

## HILLS

This is obvious when you know what it is supposed to be, but initially it can look a little puzzling. It is quite often found in Italian and Papal heraldry.

## ICEBERG

This uncommon charge is blazoned 'an iceberg proper'.

## BEACON

In this basket a fire was lit as a warning or signal and was visible from a long way off. Beacons were used as lights for navigation, as lighthouses before they existed, to warn of approaching danger or as celebration. As long as each beacon was in sight of the next, news could be spread very quickly.

## GRID IRON

An iron placed on a fire upon which to stand pots or lay meat for grilling. The common use of barbecues will have made this a familiar item to us again.

## PASSION NAILS

These are supposed to represent the nails with which Jesus was nailed to the cross.

## BATTERING RAM

In the days when defenders had the annoying habit of locking themselves inside fortified places, attackers had to resort to this instrument, wielded by as many men as were needed to lift it, to break down the door. Large ones were even constructed out of whole tree trunks and suspended on ropes in a wheeled cart including a roof to protect those with-

in from the missiles of those without. Today, small two-man versions of these are sometimes used by the police.

## COOKING POT

Used particularly in Spanish heraldry and allusive to the right and power of raising an army. This was only allowed to certain Grandees and so its use was allusive of importance.

## SPUR AND FETLOCK

The spur can still be seen today on ceremonial uniforms, but at one time it was commonly used by horsemen to urge their mounts to greater speed or more effort. It was worn strapped to the heel of the boot. The fetlock was used to fasten the two legs of a captive or beast together. One was placed on each leg and they were chained or tied together.

## CORONAL OR CRONEL

This item was placed over the point of a lance when jousting to prevent injury to the opponent. It should not be confused with a chess rook.

## PURSE

This item occasionally appears in different guises. As a pilgrim's purse it is usually shown with a staff. The great seals of a Sovereign were kept in a purse and its use might indicate one of high office.

MILLRIND

MAUNCH

CHESS ROOK

CLARION

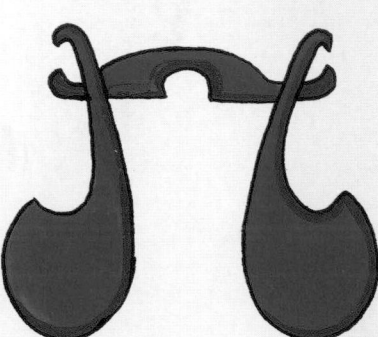

BOUGET

FLEAM

WOOLSACK

'LOZENGY TASSLED'
CUSHION

GRENADE

POMEGRANATE

HILLS

ICEBERG

BEACON

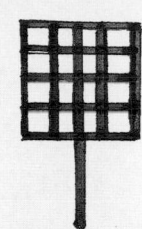

GRID IRON

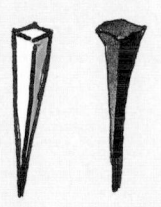

PASSION NAILS

BATTERING RAM

COOKING POT

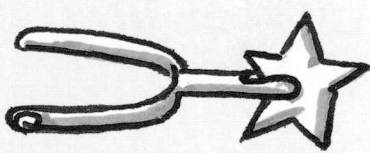

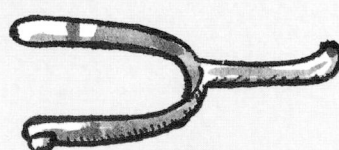

SPURS

FETLOCK

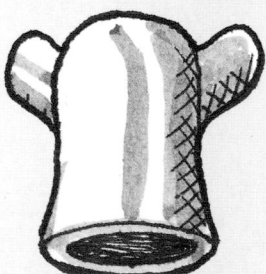

CORONAL

# Canting or Allusive Arms

This short section is about designs of arms that make a direct allusion to the name of the bearer. It would be very nice to be able to look at a coat of arms and ascertain its meaning and the reason why those particular charges have been chosen and determine what they are saying. In most instances, this is not possible as the rationale behind the composition of the achievement is not known. With canting arms there is an obvious connection and it is possible to understand the reason behind the choice of subject.

LORD FISHER OF LAMBETH has a crest a kingfisher proper, holding in its dexter claw a fleur de lys sable.

LORD GEDDES has geds (pike) as charges, supporters and on his crest.

BAYNES bears sable a shin bone in fess surmounted by another in page argent.

BULL displays sable three astronomical signs of Taurus, or.

BUTLER bears covered cups.

COOT bears argent a chevron sable between three coots, close (wings by their sides) proper.

CORBET bears or a raven (known as a corbie) sable.

METCALF bears argent three calves sable.

VEAL bears two lightning strikes in chevron between three calves.

SWINTON bears boars as charges, supporters and crest.

SHAKESPEAR bears or on a bend sable a tilting spear or.

SHEARER bears reaping hooks.

LILLY bears gules, three lilies slipped argent.

APPLEGARTH bears three apples slipped gules.

ARUNDEL bears sable six swallows (hirondels) argent.

ASPEN bears azure an aspen leaf or.

ALPE OF NORFOLK azure a fess ermine between three alpes (bullfinches) argent.

THE TOWN OF BERN bears gules a bear sable.

THE COUNTS OF BAR bear azure crusily (strewn with crosses) two barbles haurient and adorsed or.

BEAN bears gules three bean pods pendant or.

BAT bears or three bats sable.

BROCKET has as a crest a brocket (a young stag) lodged sable.

BROCK OF KENT has on a mount vert a badger sable.

THE FATHER OF ANN BOLEYN bore argent a chevron gules between three bulls heads sable armed or, though she was granted a shield of six quarters by Henry VIII which did not include this coat.

THE KINGDOM OF CASTILLE in Spain bore gules a three towered castle or.

The neighbouring KINGDOM OF LEON bore argent a lion rampant purple.

COLUMBALL bore sable three doves argent beaked and membered gules, in their beakssprigs of olive proper (*columb* means dove in Latin)

DE LA HAY bears argent the sun in splendour or.

THE DAUPHIN, the heir to the French throne, bore azure a dolphin embowed or allusive to his Dukedom, from the Celtic dalnapen which means 'district

of the chief' and became corrupted to Dauphin.

ELMS bears ermine on a bend sable, ten elm leaves or. Faisant bears azure three pheasants or, beaked and membered gules.

FIGURA OF SPAIN bears or five fig leaves in saltyre vert.

GRICE bore quarterly, gules and azure on a bend ermine, three boars passant, sable armed or. (A young boar is known as a grice.)


This gives some idea of the variety of items encountered: Herringhams bear herrings; Roach bear roaches; Lucy bears lucies (pike); Mills bear millrinds and Moore bears moorcocks. Pont bears a bridge of two arches; de Pines has three gold pine cones and Tremaynes bears three arms joined at the shoulder. Whalley bears whales.

If you know the name of the bearer, you can deduce the reason for the charge, but you cannot look at a shield and deduce from it the name of the bearer, for there may be many different reasons why those charges have been given to that person and they may have nothing to do with his name.

CHAPTER EIGHT

# Additions to Arms and Marshalling Arms

### EXAMPLES OF AUGMENTATION

*Augmentation of the coat 'azure issuant from the sinister side a hand and in base a broken fetlock argent' to be permanently impaled by the Barons de Hochpied with their own coat of 'argent between 3 crescents sable a chevron gules'.*

*Augmentation of the addition of a chief of the colours of Belgium to the de Walters family.*

*An English augmentation of a 'Canton gules a lion passant or' to the coat of More – 'ermine three greyhounds courant sable collared gules'.*

*I*N ORDER to distinguish father from son, when both were wearing the same hereditary arms, systems were developed of adding small distinguishing charges to the shield that could be removed or altered as circumstances in the family changed. Except in Scottish Heraldry, those systems have largely dropped out of use. Scotland has developed a system of adding differently tinted borders that have to be registered for each member of the family.

Some brothers changed the tinctures on their arms or altered the charges to show that, though related to the original arms, they were in fact different; but this practice, too, has largely fallen into disuse.

#### —— AUGMENTATION ——
Throughout Europe it has been the practice of monarchs to reward their subjects for valorous and noble deeds by granting to them some permanent addition to their Coat of Arms. These take many forms, but they are usually a charged canton, chief or escutcheon or even the impalement of a complete Coat of Arms.

## MARSHALLING ARMS

It is common to find more than one Coat of Arms displayed on a shield and it is important to understand how this occurs.

#### —— IMPALEMENT ——
This term refers to two Coats of Arms placed side by side on the same shield. This can happen following a marriage, when the husband's arms appear on the dexter and the wife's on the sinister side of the shield. A person can also impale his arms with the arms of any civic body of which he is the leader, during his tenure of office. The person's arms appear on the sinister and the civic arms on the dexter side of the shield.

#### —— DIMIDIATION ——
There was a time when only half of each Coat of Arms was placed on the shield. In some cases this practice produced Achievements that were totally unreadable, and it was soon dropped, though some examples still exist that are used today.

#### —— QUARTERING ——
Quartering means dividing the shield into sections, at least four and sometimes as many as

*Traditional small marks of difference, added to a coat of arms to denote a junior branch of a family.*

LEFT *The shields of the Black Prince and of his brothers, each displaying the Royal arms of England but each with a different label, differently charged.*

twenty-four. In each section a Coat of Arms is placed that has become permanently joined to the original Coat, usually by marriage to an heiress. From the Heraldic point of view, an heiress is the daughter of an armiger who has no sons. If there is more than one daughter, they are heiresses jointly and equally. Because there are no sons to carry the arms into the next generation, an heiress who marries an armiger can hand on her arms to her children as a quartering with their father's Coat. If her husband is not an armiger she cannot pass on her arms. If she is already the heiress to a quartered Coat she can pass on all or a selection of those quarterings, so long as the quartering that brought them into the family is shown. An even number of quarters is usually shown, repeating the paternal Coat in the last quarter if necessary.

Sovereigns also add quarterings to their shields, to demonstrate their sovereignty over different subject states. The Achievement of Arms on the front cover is a good example of this.

#### —— ESCUTCHEON OF PRETENCE ——

When an armiger marries an Heraldic heiress he places her arms, after her father's death, on a small escutcheon in the middle of his shield. When he dies his sons can display their father's Coat of Arms, quartered with their mother. After a few generations of marriages to heiresses, or to those who subsequently become heiresses because their brothers die, a large number of quarterings can be accumulated. It is important, though often difficult, to distinguish between two quartered Coats impaled on the same shield and one multi-quartered Coat.

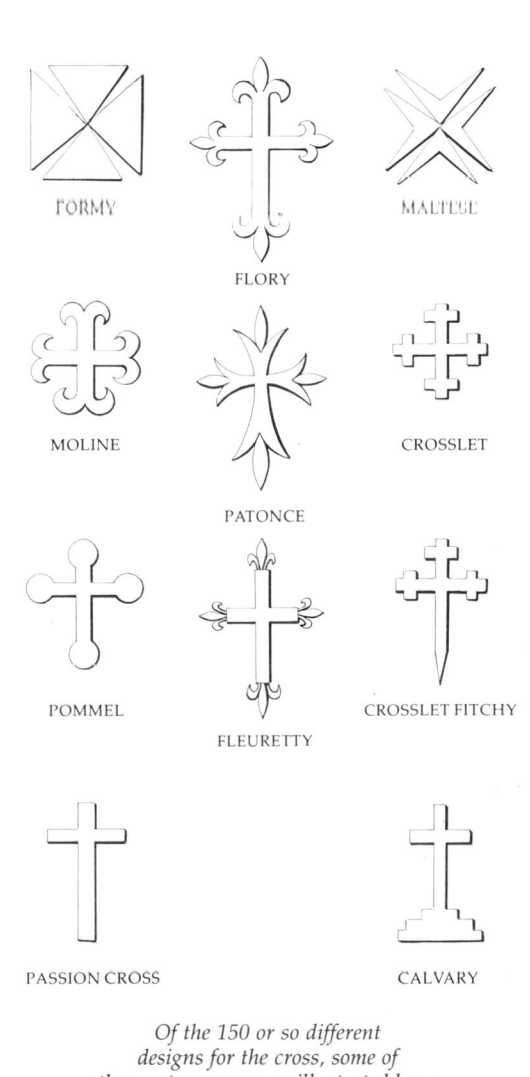

FORMY

FLORY

MALTESE

MOLINE

PATONCE

CROSSLET

POMMEL

FLEURETTY

CROSSLET FITCHY

PASSION CROSS

CALVARY

*Of the 150 or so different designs for the cross, some of the most common are illustrated here.*

# Marshalling of Arms

Earlier in this book I mentioned the occasions when two or more coats of arms are displayed on one shield especially with respect to Royal heraldry, with the intention of demonstrating sovereignty over territory. I want now to discuss the mechanisms and form for doing this with ordinary armigerous people since an understanding of this will help with the more usual displays of heraldry that you see, for example in churches, on tombs and buildings.

The first thing to consider is that heraldry is hereditary. Heraldic devices are passed down from one generation to the next. This being the case, it is important to understand how it is done.

When a son comes of age, he is entitled to display his father's coat of arms, bearing some small mark of difference (see Marks of Difference) so that it is possible to tell one from the other.. When the father dies, the first son, who has now become the head of the family removes his mark of difference and bears the un-differenced coat of arms of his father. Any other sons retain their marks of difference because their position in the family is not changed, unless the first son dies without his own heir, in which case the next son takes the place as the head of the family and bears the un-differenced coat. These coats of arms can be passed down through the generations in the respective families by the male heirs. What then if a man has only daughters? Are his arms to die with him? Quite possibly, yes. If none of the daughters marries, this will be the case. They, if there are more than one, are heiresses in heraldry of equal right and they may display their father's arms after his death until they die. The arms will then cease to have any one able to bear them and they become a matter of history. If, however, one or any of them marries, the situation is different.

If an armigerous (entitled to bear arms) man married an heraldic heiress, he may display on his shield, her arms on an 'escutcheon' (called an 'escutcheon of pretence') He has no right to the arms, he is only preserving them for his heirs. His heirs may then quarter their mother's arms with those of their father. If the parent's arms are each a simple unquartered coat, the form is to divide the shield into four sections and place the paternal coat in the first and fourth quarter and the maternal coat in the second and third quarter. If the mother already has a quartered coat these quarters are included in the third and fourth quarter and more if necessary. If the father has a quartered coat, the new quarters come after the last of the father's quarters. It is not necessary to display all the quarters, if there are many, but if any are added the mother's paternal coat must be the first. There should always be an even number of quarters and so the paternal coat is repeated in last quarter if necessary. If a daughter marries a non-armigerous husband, she may display her father's arms until she dies, but there is no vehicle for its continuance into the next generation and so the arms die with her. It is

quite incorrect for her children to display her arms, or use inherited rings, etc., though they often do. There is one course open and that is to apply to the College of Arms for a Grant of Arms to the husband, in his own right. Once this has been done, he can display the wife's arms on his own on an escutcheon of pretence and bear them forward for the next generation.

If a woman has brothers, she is not a heraldic heiress and she cannot carry her paternal arms forward, this is already being done by her brothers. However, her husband can impale her arms (place them side by side on the same shield) with his own if this is desirable. Such arms may not be carried forward by the next generation and the impalement ends with the generation for whom it was done.

It is quite common to see arms impaled with civic arms or of other arms pertaining to an office, particularly with Bishops, who display the arms of their See on the dexter side of their shield and their paternal arms on the sinister side. If they wish to display their wife's arms as an impalement they should marshall together a second shield showing their paternal arms on the dexter side and wife's paternal arms on the sinister side.

## DEXTER AND SINISTER

These two Latin terms mean right (dexter) and left (sinister). Left and right in heraldry are slightly confusing. They are always taken to be from the point of view of the person bearing and so standing behind the shield, so when you, the observer, stand looking at the shield, that which is known as dexter appears to you to be on the left. When impaling coats, the most important goes on the dexter side.

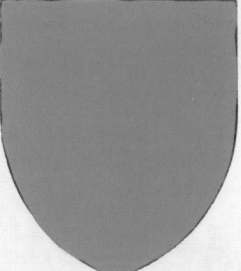

ARMS OF THE
FATHER

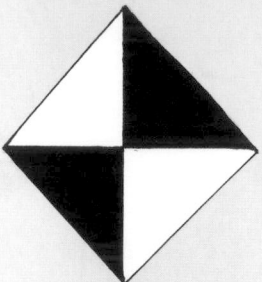

ARMS OF HIS WIFE
WHO IS A HERALDIC
HEIRESS

THE HUSBAND
BEARS HER ARMS
ON HIS OWN AS AN
ESCUTCHEON OF
PRETENCE

THEIR HEIRS MAY
QUARTER THE
MOTHER'S ARMS
WITH THOSE OF
THE FATHER

ARMS OF THE FIRST-BORN SON IF
HIS MOTHER WAS NOT
A HERALDIC HEIRESS, HE BEARS
HIS FATHER'S ARMS ONLY WITH A
MARK OF DIFFERENCE

A MAN WHOSE WIFE IS NOT A HERALDIC HEIRESS MAY
IMPALE HER ARMS WITH HIS OWN

ARMS OF THE
HUSBAND

HIS WIFE'S
ARMS IMPALED
WITH THOSE OF
HIS OWN

IF A MAN TAKES A POSITION THAT INCLUDES ITS OWN COAT OF
ARMS, HE MAY IMPALE THEM WITH THOSE OF HIS OWN

ARMS OF A MAN
BEFORE BECOMING
A BISHOP

ARMS OF HIS SEE
IMPALED WITH
THOSE OF HIS OWN

# Scottish System of Differencing Arms

The Scottish system for differencing arms for junior branches of the family calls for permitant additions and alterations to the coat of arms and these have to be approved and registered by the appropriate heraldic authorities in Scotland, whose advice should always be sought.

The system is relatively straightforward. From the diagram it will be seen that a father has five sons. The eldest displays a label that can be removed when he in his turn becomes the head of the family. The other sons difference their arms by employing a different coloured bordure. Their sons display the bordure of their father to maintain their differences from the senior branch and in addition they use different lines of partition so that for each one of them, the shield is unique.

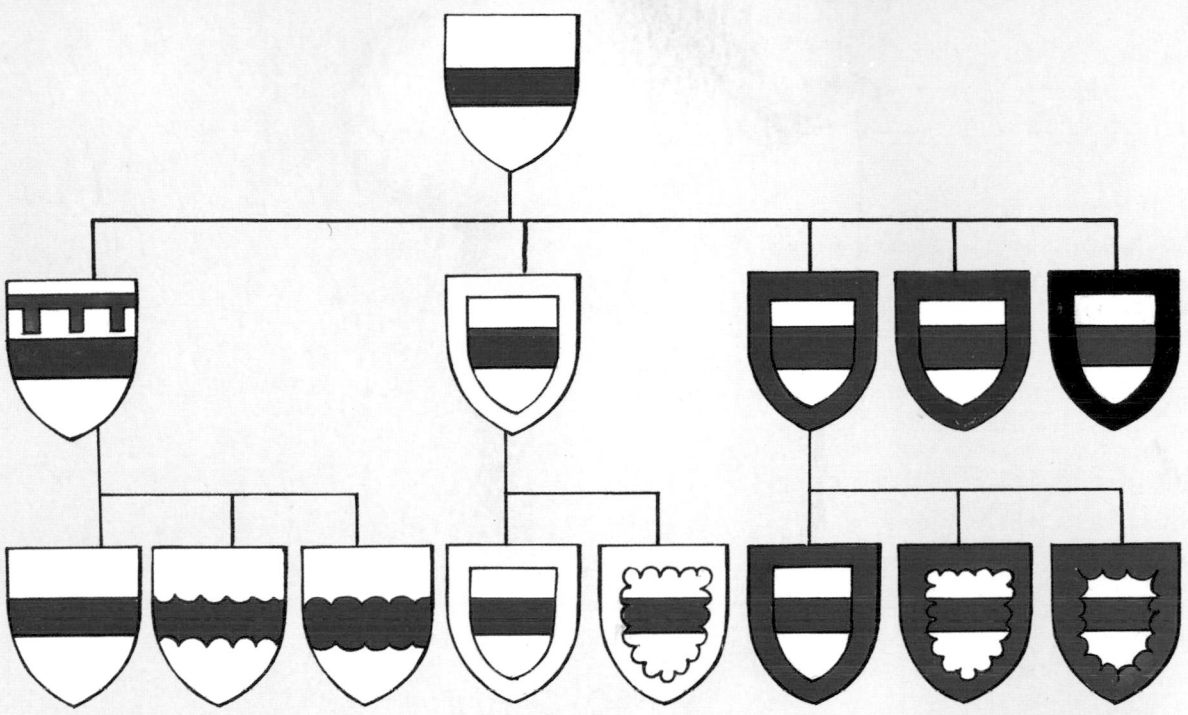

THE SCOTTISH SYSTEM OF DIFFERENCING ARMS FOR JUNIOR BRANCHES OF THE FAMILY

CHAPTER NINE

# Ecclesiastical Heraldry

ERALDIC-LIKE devices have been used by churches since the beginning of Christianity. Ecclesiastical establishments have been granted land by the sovereign or, through piety or the desire to expiate sins, by landowners. Since the earliest times, therefore, they have had to fulfil the role of lord of the manor. Consequently, they have needed to use seals, badges and other devices to identify themselves and their retainers. These devices developed along Heraldic lines over the centuries and, although different denominations have different traditions, some general comments can be made.

## EPISCOPAL HERALDRY

A bishop, who has authority over a number of priests in an area called a diocese, can, like the holder of a civic office, impale his personal arms, if he has them, with the official arms of his diocese. He places the diocesan arms on the dexter side of his shield and his own on the sinister side. On the Continent it is quite common for a bishop to quarter his arms with those of his see. He may also place a mitre over his shield and display behind it a crozier, or two in saltire, or an episcopal staff, as an emblem of his episcopal authority.

A number of terms in episcopal Heraldry deserve notice.

**CROZIER** This ceremonial staff, based on the shepherd's crook, symbolizes the episcopal authority of a bishop. It has a crook to gather in the lost, a stout staff to hold up the weak and a point to goad the reluctant!

**EPISCOPAL HAT** This is a flat hat with a wide brim, a shallow crown and pendant tassels. It is used in different colours and with different numbers of tassels to indicate the rank of the cleric.

**EPISCOPAL STAFF** This has a function similar to that of a crozier, but has a cross (of varying types) on the head instead of a crook.

Cardinals, who are of a higher rank than bishops, can display over their arms a red hat with tassels, fifteen on each side. If they are also bishops they can show under their hat a mitre and a crozier.

**MITRES** The mitre can take a variety of forms within two broad categories — completely plain, 'mitre simplex', or heavily decorated and jewelled. 'mitre preciosa'. Instead of displaying a mitre shown over his arms, a bishop may show a green episcopal hat with green tassels hanging down on both sides of the shield.

As a matter of style, the Catholic Church now favours an Achievement showing the episcopal arms with an ecclesiastical hat placed above and a staff placed behind. Anglican churches place a gold mitre and crossed croziers behind the arms. Eastern churches use the eastern forms of mitre and staff.

## —— PAPAL HERALDRY ——

Popes, like other high dignitaries of the Church, have frequently used the horsehead-shaped shield, which looks less military and therefore is more suited to a man of God. For the same reason, it is not now felt appropriate for a cleric of any rank to display a crest and helm; hence the adoption of different orders of the clerical hat.

Papal heraldry has also adopted other symbols.

**TIARA** The tiara is the triple crown of the pope. The shape of the hat on which the three crowns are placed has long been considered an emblem of liberty and the three crowns are said to symbolize the pope's supremacy over the Church militant, the Church penitent and the Church triumphant. They also symbolize his three roles as priest, pastor and teacher.

**CROSSED KEYS OF ST. PETER** These are always shown with the tiara as a symbol of the papacy and are commonly placed on a red shield. A pope will place the tiara over the papal arms and the crossed keys behind his personal arms. The keys symbolize the power to bind or lock in and to set free or loose.

## —— OTHER ECCLESIASTICAL —— SYMBOLS

**UMBALINO OR PAVILION** This is shown as an umbrella, or tent, with a red and gold striped cover. It is used as the emblem of a basilica in the Catholic Church.

With crossed keys it is used as the emblem of authority of the cardinal in charge ('Camerlengo') in an interregnum between popes. When placed with the cross keys behind, it has been used by Italian families in association with their arms to indicate that they have had a pope in the family.

**PALLIUM** This is a band of cloth, worn about the shoulders, charged with black crosses and two pendant strips. It is a symbol of authority given by the pope to an archbishop, who cannot commence his office until he receives it. It is displayed wherever it is possible to arrange it satisfactorily with the Achievement. It may be found as a charge on a shield, as it is in the Archdiocese of Canterbury.

**ROSARY** This string of beads, ten and one repeated five times, used to count repeated contemplative prayers, is sometimes found around a shield. It was used by a knight who had taken religious vows.

LEFT *The arms of a cardinal traditionally display the red cardinal's hat with 15 tassels on each side.*

BELOW LEFT *The arms of the Anglican Bishop of Ely: the gold mitre is in the Anglican style, but in this case there are no crossed croziers, which are usually displayed behind the arms.*

BELOW RIGHT *The arms of a bishop often display a green episcopal hat with tassels instead of a mitre.*

# Orders of Chivalry and Entitlement to Arms

IT HAS long been the custom for sovereigns to instigate orders of chivalry to honour the nation's most distinguished men. These orders have emblems that the members wear and which appear on their Achievements. Practice varies widely from country to country and it is beyond the scope of this book to go into the subject in great detail.

CIRCLET European knights of an order often place a circlet around a shield. It is usually shown with a motto, as, for example, in the British Order of the Garter, which is blue with a gold edge and buckle and has the motto, 'Honi soit qui mal y pense'. — 'Evil be to he who evil thinks'.

CHAIN This is usually called a collar, a gold chain worn around the arms, with the emblems of the order in alternate links and the badge of the order pendant, as, for example, in the Swedish Order of the Seraphim. People may display collars of more than one order. Care should be taken with chains, as some officers of state also display a chain.

BADGE The badge of an order is displayed by lower-ranking members of the order on a riband, below the shield.

## RELIGIOUS ORDERS OF CHIVALRY

These are survivors of the Crusades, when knights joined the military and hospital orders to fight for the Holy Lands and care for the sick and wounded soldiers and pilgrims. Some of these continue to exist for philanthropic purposes. They have their own arms and badges, known as crosses.

Grandmasters can show the arms of the order on their shields as a chief or quartering. Knights and dames of the order display the cross of their order behind the shield. Members can hang the cross of the order on a riband of the order below the shield.

## ENTITLEMENT TO ARMS

Anyone may apply for a new grant of Arms, but a person is entitled to existing arms only if he can prove that he is descended in the male line from someone to whom a grant of arms had previously been made. Some countries permit people to assume arms at will, but there is then no guarantee that the arms are unique.

Heraldry is essentially a European phenomenon. Because Heraldic authorities in Europe have jurisdiction only over citizens of their own country, anyone wishing to enquire into their Heraldic status should of course apply to the authority in his own country.

In the New World the position is slightly different. Many of the peoples of those countries are of European stock. If a person wishes to prove his right to an existing Coat of Arms, he must apply to his country of origin or that of his ancestors. If he seeks a new Coat of Arms, he must apply to his own country. Heralds of one country cannot grant Coats of Arms to citizens of another, though they can make 'devisals of arms' to such people, which are then registered and recorded.

# Modern Usage

THE variety of ways in which Heraldic bearings can be displayed, their decorative function and intriguing rules of form, have ensured the survival of this unique art form. The ownership of a Coat of Arms, whether it be one long in the family or one newly granted, is a matter of justified pride, a pride that can be expressed by displaying and using the arms in a wide variety of ways. Provided that they are employed with good taste, their use can only enhance the appearance of personal items and artefacts. Artists and craftsmen and some agencies specialize in supplying work of an Heraldic nature.

It is very important, when commissioning Heraldic work, to make sure that the artist is a competent exponent of Heraldic art who will render the work both artistically and correctly. Heraldry is not a representational art. The task of the Heraldic artist is to convey a brief message by using symbols. It is the symbolism of the items that he is trying to portray, not the actual item. He has to work with full regard to historical precedent and style, without forgetting that he is an artist of his own time.

It is worth going to a specialist agency which will be eager to meet both these ends and which will have on hand competent craftsmen who can undertake work in all kinds of media.

ON CHINA Painted and fired armorial painting and decoration.

ON CLOTH Painted, printed and sewn flags, banners and standards. Embroidered fire screens, stool and seat covers, chair backs. Painted and printed bedspreads. Sewn spinnaker sails for yachts. Heraldic costumes.

ON GLASS Engraved on table glass, doors and windows, table tops and firescreens. Stained-glass windows and hanging plaques. Lamp windows.

ON JEWELLERY Engraved rings, seals, personal items. Cast sculptured items, car mascots. Enamelled and jewelled cuff links, badges and brooches, pendants. Enamelled box lids and wall plaques.

ON LEATHER Embossed and gilded book bindings and covers, desk sets and chairbacks, boxes and belts.

ON PAPER AND VELLUM Paintings of Heraldic Achievements, illuminated and calligraphic illustrations, family trees, book plates in black and white and in full colour.

ON WOOD Wall plaques, carved, and gilded or painted. Carved newel posts, carved, painted and gilded backs and panels on furniture. Carved and painted or gilded shields.

# Glossary

## A

**ABBESS** The senior member, or superior of a female religious house.

**ABBEY** A building housing a society of monks or nuns. Also the society itself.

**ABBOT** The senior member, or superior, of a male religious house.

**ACHIEVEMENT OF ARMS** The complete assemblage of Heraldic accessories assigned to an individual, corporation or state.

**ACORNED** Of the acorns of an oak, in separate specified colour.

**ADDORSED** Of beasts or charges, back-to-back.

**AFFRONTY** Of a *charge*, facing the observer.

**ANGLED** Of a *line of partition*, set at an angle.

**APAUMY** Of a hand or gauntlet, open to show the palm.

**ARCH (ARCHY)** Of a *line of partition*, in the form of an arch.

**ARGENT** The colour silver or white, a *tincture* of Heraldry; a *metal*.

**ARMED** Of a human being or limb clothed in armour; the claws, beak, horns or tusks of a creature, in a separate, specified colour.

**ARMET** A totally enclosed, close-fitting helmet with opening front.

**ARMIGER** A person entitled to bear arms.

**ARMORIAL** A book listing *armorial bearings* alphabetically by the names of the bearers.

**ARMORIAL BEARINGS** The symbols born by an *armiger* his *coat armour*, *shield* and *banner* to distinguish him from others.

**ARTISTIC SUPPORTER** *Supporter* with no Heraldic significance, added for effect.

**ATTRIBUTED ARMS** *Armorial bearings* given to people who existed before Heraldry and to celestial and legendary figures.

**AUGMENTATION** An additional charge or device awarded to an *armiger* as a reward for merit in some field or to commemorate a special event.

**AZURE** The colour blue, a *tincture* of Heraldry.

## B

**BADGE** An Heraldic device belonging to an *armiger*, worn by his retainers and sympathizers.

**BANNER** A square or rectangular flag upon which *armorial bearings* are displayed.

**BAR** A narrow strip on the *shield* in a horizontal plane ('barry', with several such strips).

**BARS GEMEL** Horizontal bars, arranged in pairs.

**BASILISK** An Heraldic monster, a reptile said to be hatched by a serpent from a cock's egg.

**BATH, KNIGHTS OF THE** Active order of knights in Great Britain, in civil and military divisions.

**BATTLED (EMBATTLED)** Of a *line of partition*, having a crenellated edge like a battlement.

**BATON** A narrow, diagonal band not reaching the edge of the *shield*, in England sometimes in the form of the baton sinister, a mark of illegitimacy.

**BEAKED** Of a beak, in a separate specified colour.

**BELLED** With bells, attached to a hawk's leg for hawking, in a separate specified colour.

**BEND** A diagonal strip on the *shield* from *sinister* to *dexter* top; an *ordinary* 'per bend', divided in the same plane; 'In bend', charges placed in this plane.

**BEND SINISTER** A diagonal strip on the *shield* from *dexter* to *sinister* top.

**BENDLET** A narrow *bend*.

**BENDY** Covered with an even number of *bends*.

**BEVELLED** Of a *line of partition*, broken so as to have two equally acute, alternate angles.

**BEZANT (BYZANT)** A gold *roundle* representing a coin.

**BEZANTY** Covered with gold coins.

**BICORPORATE** Two bodies joined to one head.

**BILLET** A rectangular shape, placed on end, representing a block of wood, usually used in large numbers to cover a *field*.

**BILLETY** Covered with billets.

**BLAZON** The written description of *armorial bearings* 'to blazon' is to describe armorial bearings in words.

**BLEU CÉLESTE** The colour sky blue, a *ticture* of Heraldry.

**BONICON** A mythical beast.

**BORDURE** A narrow band around the edge of the *shield*.

**BOTONY** With ends like a clover leaf.

**BOUGET** Two water carriers hanging from a yoke.

## C

**CABOSHED** Of a head, front-facing and cut off behind the ears.

**CADENCE** The difference between the main bearer of arms in a family and cadet, or junior branches; a system of small additions and alterations to the *shield* to show this.

**CALTRAP (CALTROP)** A spiked device strewn on the ground to maim horses, used as a *charge*.

**CALVARY CROSS** One of the forms of the cross, shown on three steps.

**CANTING** *Armorial bearings* that in their concept and design include some reference or allusion to the name of the bearer.

**CANTON** A square section, smaller than a *quartering* in the top dexter or sinister corner of the shield; a *sub-ordinary*.

**CENTAUR** A monster, half man and half horse.

**CELESTIAL CROWN** An Heraldic *crown*.

**CHAIN** Separate links appearing as *charges*; sometimes a chain of office or of an order; when it is known as *collars*.

**CHAPEAU** A hat with a turned-up lining of *fur*, placed over the *helm* on which the *crest* stands; symbolic of especial dignity.

**CHARGE** Any device placed upon a *shield* or upon another item.

**CHEQUEY (CHECKY)** Of a *shield* or *charge*, covered all over with equal-sized squares, in two alternating colours, set in many rows.

**CHERUB** The lowest order of the heavenly host; shown as a boy's face over two wings.

**CHEVALIER** A rank in French-speaking countries, equivalent to an English knight or German ritter.

**CHEVRON** A V-shaped strip, inverted, an *ordinary* ('Per chevron', the *field* or any area of colour divided as by a chevron).

**CHEVRONELS** A bent bar on an escutcheon, half the breadth of the *chevron*; a small chevron.

**CHIEF** The top section of the *shield*; an *ordinary*; ('in chief', of *charges* placed in this area on a shield).

**CINQUEFOIL** A stylized flower, with five petals.

**CIRCLET** A riband placed around a *shield* bearing a motto, usually of one of the orders of knighthood.

**CLOSE** Of a winged creature, when standing on the ground with its wings shut.

**COAT ARMOUR** A heavy, flowing, padded coat worn by knights to protect them from sword cuts, on which were painted their *armorial bearings*.

**COAT OF ARMS** A synonymous term for *coat armour*; now come to mean that which was painted on the coat, the *armorial bearings*. Because these are nowadays shown on a *shield*, a shield with armorial bearings painted on it is known as a Coat of Arms.

**COCKATRICE** A mythological Heraldic monster, synonymous with a *basilisk*.

**COILED** Of a snake, ready to strike.

**COLLAR** A chain of office of one of the orders of knighthood.

**COLLARED** Of a beast with a collar around its neck; synonymous with 'gorged'; not a chain of an order, unless specified.

**COLLEGE OF ARMS** The building in London where English Heralds have their chambers.

**COLOURS** The *tinctures* of Heraldry that represent red, blue, green, black and purple.

**COMBATANT** Two beasts or humans fighting each other.

**COMPARTMENT** A representation of the ground or whatever on which the *supporters*, *shield* and motto stand.

**COMPONY** Of a row of squares of two alternating colours, synonymous with 'gobony'. See *counter company* and *chequey*.

**CORONEL** Crown-shaped tip of a lance, used in jousting to prevent injury.

**CORONET** A *metal*, decorated headwear, symbolic of rank.

**COTISE** A narrow band placed outside, and separate from, a wider band; can be found in multiples, specified; 'double cottice' should not be confused with *bar gemel*.

**COUCHANT** Of an animal, lying down with head erect.

**COUNTER** Opposite.

**COUNTER-CHANGED** A *charge* placed upon a divided field with the *tinctures* reversed.

**COUNTER-COMPANY** Of two rows of differently coloured square sections arranged alternately.

**COUPED** Of anything, cut off cleanly, for example an arm, head or branch.

**COWED** Of a beast, with its tail between its legs.

**CRESCENT** A representation of the moon, shown with both horns upright (see also *increscent* and *decrescent*).

**CREST** A decorative accessory placed on the helmet.

**CRESTED** Of the *crest*, in a separate specified colour.

**CRINED** With head-hair or mane, in a separate specified colour.

**CROSS** 1 A horizontal and vertical band, each of the same colour, placed centrally on a *shield*; an *ordinary*; ('per cross', the *field* of the shield divided horizontally and vertically into four equal parts, synonymous with 'quarterly'; 'in cross', repeated *charges* placed upon a shield in a cross formation).

2 A charge on the shield representing a cross.

**CROSSLET** A small cross with the end of each arm itself crossed.

**CROWN (HERALDIC)** A symbolic *charge* used to denote an interest in a particular activity.

**CROZIER** A ceremonial staff, symbolizing the role of a shepherd, used by a bishop.

**CRUSILY** Covered all over with little crosses.

**CUBIT ARM** An arm cut off cleanly between the hand and the elbow.

**CUFFED** Of the turned-up cuff of a sleeve, in its separate specified colour.

## D

**DANCY** Of a *line of partition*, toothed or indented.

**DECRESCENT** Of a *crescent*, facing sinister.

**DEVICE** An artistic, traditional or Heraldic symbol (or symbols) chosen to represent a person.

**DEVISAL** A unique design of *armorial bearings* devised and recorded by a Herald in one country for a citizen of another.

**DEXTER** Right, considered from the point of view of the person bearing the *shield*, thus standing behind it.

**DIAPERING** A pattern in tone, on a plain *field*, to represent brocade; sometimes worked in gold paint.

**DIMIDIATION** The practice whereby half of one *Coat of Arms* is impaled (see impalement) on a shield with half of another Coat of Arms.

**DIMINUTIVE** Smaller, often multiple, version of an *ordinary* or *sub-ordinary*.

**DISARMED** Of a creature, without his beak, claws, teeth or tusks.

**DISPLAYED** Of a winged creature, spread out on the *shield*.

**DORMANT** Of a creature, asleep.

**DOUBLE-ARCHED** Of a *line of partition*.

**DOUBLE-QUEUED** Of a creature, with two tails.

**DOVETAILED** Of a *line of partition*.

## E

**ELEVATED** Of a bird with his wings out, the tips raised.

**EMBLAZON** To draw or paint a *Coat of Arms* in full colour.

**EMBLAZONED** Of a *Coat of Arms*, shown in pictorial form.

**ENARCHED** Of a *line of partition* having an arch in its inner angle.

**ENGRAILED** Of a *line of partition*, curvilinearly hotched.

**ERADICATED** Of a plant or tree, pulled up, roots and all, from the ground.

**ERASED** Of a limb of a human being or creature, or any part of an entity, as if pulled off the main body, leaving a jagged edge.

**ERECT** Of any item, placed upright.

**ERMINE** Of the *tinctures* of Heraldry, one of the *Furs*; white with black 'tails'.

**ERMINES** Of the tinctures of Heraldry, one of the *Furs*; black with white 'tails'.

**ERMINOIS** Of the tinctures of Heraldry, one of the *furs*; gold with black 'tails' (see *pean*).

**ESCARTELED** Of a *line of partition*, having square hotches.

**ESCUTCHEON** A *shield*, usually small, used as a *charge* upon another.

**ESCUTCHEON OF PRETENCE** A small *shield* bearing the arms of an heiress placed upon the shield of her husband's arms.

**ESTOIL** A representation of a star, with six wavy points or rays.

## F

**FACE** A creature's head *affronty* cut off cleanly behind the ears.

**FALCHION** A broad-bladed, straight sword with one side curved.

**FEATHER** One of the coverings of a bird, used as a *charge* and *crest*.

**FETTERLOCK** A removable shackle around the feet of a creature or person.

**Fesse** A horizontal strip across the middle of the *shield*; an *ordinary*; ('per fesse', the *field* divided horizontally into two equal parts; 'in fess', *charges* placed on the shield in this position).

**Fesse-wise** *Charges* placed in a horizontal plane.

**Fesse-point** The mid-point of *shield*.

**Field** The colour that the *shield* is painted before anything is placed upon it, and the divisions of this, if more than one *tincture* is used.

**Fimbriated** Of a *charge* with a strong outline of a different *tincture*.

**Fitchy** With a point, so that it can be stuck in the ground, especially of a cross.

**Flaunches** Two semi-circular sections on the sides of a *shield*, of a different *tincture* from the *field*.

**Fleur de lis** A stylized form, in many varieties, of the lily.

**Fleuretty** Of a cross, from the ends issuing in *fleurs de lis*.

**Flory (fleury)** 1. With the ends terminating in *fleurs de lis*.
2. Of a *line of partition* decorated thus.

**Formy** Of a cross made with wide triangular pieces, meeting at the centre.

**Fountain** A *roundle* with white and blue wavy lines.

**Fraise (frase, fraze)** A white *cinquefoil* representing the strawberry flower, from the French, *fraise*.

**Fret** Two diagonal strips interlacing a void diamond shape, said to represent the knot of a fishing net.

**Fretty** Covered with interwoven diagonal lines from both directions.

**Fructed** Of the fruit a plant or tree, in separate specified colour.

**Fusil** An elongated diamond shape.

**Furs** The *tinctures* in Heraldry that represent fur.

───────── G ─────────

**Garb** A sheaf of wheat or other grain-bearing plant; also applied to arrows or anything else shown in bundles.

**Garter, the** A blue garter, worn below the knee, bearing the motto, 'Honi soit qui mal y pense', 'Evil be to he who evil thinks,' by Knights of the Garter; also displayed around their shields.

**Garter, Order of** The oldest and senior order of knighthood still existing in England.

**Gentleman** An untitled person entitled to bear arms.

**Glade** A spear with serrated inner edges for catching eels and other fish.

**Gobony** See *compony*.

**Golpe** A mulberry-coloured *roundle*, representing a wound.

**Gonfanon** A long flag, suspended from the top and hanging vertically having long tails.

**Gorged** See *collared*.

**Goutte (gutte)** A small, drop-shaped figure of specified *tincture*, used as a *charge*.

**Goutty** Covered with small, drop-shaped figures.

**Grady** Of a *line of partition*, stepped.

**Grant of arms** A Formal document giving sole right to a person and his heirs to bear arms, granted by a competent authority.

**Griffin (gryphon)** A mythical beast, having the head and wings of an eagle and the body and hind quarters of a lion.

**Guardant** Of a creature or human, looking out of the *shield* at the observer.

**Gules** Of the *tinctures* of Heraldry, the colour red.

**Gunstone** A black *roundle*, also known as a *pellate*.

**Gyron** A wedge-shaped *charge*, placed in the lower diagonal half of a *canton*.

**Gyrony** Of wedge-shaped sections, formed by diagonal, vertical and horizontal lines, crossing in the centre.

───────── H ─────────

**Habited** Of clothes, with a specified colour or type; synonymous with 'vested'.

**Hand of Ulster** A red hand, palm showing, on a white *shield*, the *badge* of a baronet.

**Harpy** A monster, having a woman's face and body and a bird's wings and claws.

**Hart** A full-grown red deer stag.

**Hatchment** A diamond-shaped board with *armorial bearings* painted for the funeral of the bearer.

**Haurient** Of a fish, swimming to the top of the *shield*.

**Hawking** Favourite sport of the Middle Ages, in which a trained bird of prey was used to catch game.

**Heater** A shape of *shield*, resembling a flat iron.

**Helm** Heraldic term for a helmet.

**Horned** With horns, in a separate specified colour.

───────── I ─────────

**Impalement** The practice of placing two, sometimes three, *Coats of Arms* side by side on the same shield.

**Incensed** Issuing flames or vapour.

**Increscent** Of a *crescent*, facing *dexter*.

**Indented** Of a *line of partition*, having a series of similar indentations or notches.

**Infula** Ribands hanging from the back of the papal *tiara* or a bishop's mitre; derived originally from a long band tied around the head and hanging down the back.

**Invected (invecked)** Of a *line of partition*, having a series of small convex lobes.

**Inverted** Of a winged creature, with the wings open, the tips downward.

**Issuant** Of a *charge*, when it comes out of another underneath it, or from off the borders of the *shield*.

───────── J ─────────

**Jessant de lis** Of a face, placed before a *fleur de lis* with the lower part of the fleur thrust up through the mouth.

**Jessed** Of the jesses trying a bell to a falcon's leg, in a separate specified colour.

**Jousting** Organized combat between mounted knights for pageantry, display, prowess and training.

───────── K ─────────

**King of arms** The senior Herald in a country.

**Knight** One elevated to this rank and admitted to one of the orders of knighthood by the competent authority in recognition of deeds of valour or great service; a non-hereditary rank; 'Ritter' in Germany, 'chevalier' in France.

**Knot** Loops of interlaced cord frequently used as *badges* or *charges*.

───────── L ─────────

**Label** A strip across the top section of the *shield*, with pendant tabs; usually a sign of a son, by common usage the heir.

**Lambrequin** Synonymous with *mantelling*.

**Langued** Of the tongue, in a separate specified colour.

**Leaved** Of the leaves of a plant, in a separate colour.

**Ledger stone** A memorial slab placed in the floor of a church.

**Line of partition** See *partition*. Lines drawn to delineate divisions and *charges* can be of many different configurations.

**Lioncel** A small lion, used to describe one of many on one *shield*.

**Livery** The uniform worn by a lord's retainers, bearing his colours.

**Livery company** Originally a medieval trade guild, nowadays involved in charitable works.

**Lodged** Of a deer, lying down.

**Lozenge** A diamond-shaped piece. See also *mascule* and *rustre*.

**Lozengy** Of an all-over lozenge pattern, made by crossing diagonal lines.

**Lymphad** A small sailing vessel, with one sail, sometimes furled, and sometimes with oars.

───────── M ─────────

**Mace** (Battle) A spiked iron ball on a shaft, wielded in the hand, the ball sometimes attached by a short length of chain.
(Ceremonial) A large ornamental item, often with an orb and crown on top as symbol of civic authority.

**Mantelling** A short cloth attached to the back of the helmet to keep off the sun's heat and protect against sword cuts.

**Mandrake** A human monster, formed from the root of the plant of the same name.

**Marshalling** The practice of combining two or more Coats of Arms on a *shield* or in one *Achievement*.

**Martlet** A bird of the swift order, shown with no feet.

**Mascule** A *lozenge*-shaped figure, voided in the middle. See also *rustre*.

**Maunch** Representation of a sleeve, with a long pendant pocket from the wrist.

**Melusine** A human, female monster, with two fish tails.

**Mermaid** A human, female monster with a fish tail.

**Merman** A human, male monster with a fish tail

**Metal** Of the *tinctures* of Heraldry, the colours that represent silver and gold.

**Mill-rind** Iron bracket to take the spindle in the centre of a millstone to prevent wear.

**Moline** One of the forms of the cross, the arms terminating in curved branches resembling the ends of a *mill-rind*.

**Mollet (mullet)** A five-pointed *star* shape, not to be confused with a star (see *estoil*); when pierced representing a *spur rowel*.

**Moon** Shown either full, with a human face, to differentiate it from a *plate* or as a *crescent*. See also *increscent* and *decrescent*.

**Mural** An Heraldic *crown*, in embattled form.

**Murrey** One of the *tinctures* of Heraldry, a purple or red *stain*.

───────── N ─────────

**Naiant** Of fish, swimming across the *shield*, heads to the dexter.

**National arms** *Armorial bearings* used by countries, expressing territorial allegiance.

**Naval crown** One of the Heraldic crowns.

**Navel point** The lower middle point of a *shield*, below the *fessee point*.

**Nebuly** Of a *line of partition*, of a wavy or serpentine form.

**Nowed** Knotted, of a rope, a tail, a snake etc.

───────── O ─────────

**Octofoil** A flower with eight petals.

**Ogress** A black *roundle*, synonymous with *gunstone*.

**Opinicus** An Heraldic beast, the same as the griffin, but with *four* lion's legs.

**Or** Of the *tinctures* representing *metals*, the colour gold.

**Ordinary** The principal geometric *charge* on a *shield*.

**Ordinary of arms** A book listing *armorial bearings* alphabetically according to the principal *charges*, so that the bearers of arms can be ascertained by reference to the description.

**Orle** A narrow band on the *shield*, following its shape, but set in from the edge; ('in orle', *charges* placed upon a shield in the disposition of an orle).

**Ounce** A mythical beast resembling a leopard, in Heraldry often a black panther.

**Overall** Of a *charge* placed on a *shield* on top of whatever is on the shield already.

───────── P ─────────

**Pairle** A division of the *field* into three radiant sections.

**Pale** An *ordinary*, being a vertical stripe or band in the middle of the *shield*; ('in pale' *charges* placed in a vertical alignment on the shield; 'per pale', one of the divisions of the field).

**Palewise** Of *charges* placed on the *shield* vertically.

**Palisado** An Heraldic *crown*, resembling a palisade.

**Pall** A Y-shaped band, in three ships, placed upon a *shield*, derived from the *pallium*.

**Pallet** A very narrow *pale*.

**Pallium** A narrow, ring-like band of cloth lying over the shoulders, symbolizing the authority of an archbishop.

**Paly** Of the *field*, divided into an equal number of vertical strips.

**Paly bendy** Of the *field*, divided into sections by vertical and diagonal lines.

**Paper heraldry** Derogatory term applied to Heraldic accessories designed after the practical function of heraldry had passed, which could never have been used for their apparent purpose.

**Passant** Of a creature, walking across the *shield*.

**Passion cross** One of the forms of the cross; the standard crucifix.

**Patonce** One of the forms of the cross, having its arms extending in a curved form from the centre.

**Patriarchial cross** One of the forms of the cross, having two transverse arms, the upper one being the shorter.

**Pavilion** A figure in the shape of a tent, or umbrella, used as a *charge*; especially in ecclesiastical Heraldry; also called an 'umbrellino'.

**Pean** One of the Heraldic *tinctures* that represent the *furs*, black with gold spots.

**Pegasus** A horse monster, having wings.

**Pellate** A black *roundle*, synonymous with *ogress* and *gunstone*.

**Pellaty** Covered with pellates.

**Penned** See *guilled*.

**Pennon** A small pointed flag fixed at the lance point.

**Peon** A broad arrowhead, the inside edge serrated.

**Phoenix** A mythical bird.

**Pierced** Of a *charge* with a hole in it through which can be seen the colour of whatever lies underneath, unless otherwise specified.

**Pile** A triangular piece from the top of the *shield*, point towards the bottom.

**Pile bendy** A horizontal pile, with its base to *sinister*, its point to *dexter*.

**Pilgrim staff** A staff with a hook near the top to carry a pilgrim 's bag.

**Plate** A *roundle*, silver or white.

**Platy** Covered with *plates*.

**Pommel** One of the forms of the cross in which each arm terminates in a roundle.

**Pomme** A green *roundle*, representing an apple.

**Portcullis** A defensive grid dropped down in a doorway to keep out intruders.

**Potent** One of the tinctures representing the *furs*, formed of or terminating in crutch-heads.

**Potent** One of the forms of the cross, the arms terminating in potents, or crutch-heads.

**Potenty** Of a *line of partition*, formed by a series of potents, or crutch heads.

**Powdered** Covered all over with small *charges*.

**Pride, in his** A bird such as a peacock or turkey with his tail spread is said to be 'in his pride'.

**Profile** Of a human face, facing the *dexter*.

**Proper** Of anything in Heraldry *blazoned* in its natural colour.

**Purpure** Of the *tinctures* of Heraldry, purple.

### Q

**Quarter** The top dexter quarter on a *shield*.

**Quartering** One of any number of divisions on a shield, on which are placed different *Coats of Arms*.

**Quarter-pierced** Of a cross form on the *shield*, the centre removed to show the colour of the *field*, so that all the remaining cross-sections and all the field sections are as near equal as possible.

**Quatrefoil** A stylized flower with four petals, representing the poppy.

**Queue fourchy** Of the forked tail of a creature.

**Quilled** Of the shaft of a feather, synonymous with 'penned'.

### R

**Raguly** A *line of partition*, having alternate projections and depressions like a battlement, but set obliquely.

**Rampant** Of a creature, reared up to fight.

**Rayonné** A *line of partition*, having alternating pointed projections and depressions with wavy edges.

**Reflexed** Of a lead or chain on a creature, bent over the back and down to the ground.

**Reguardant** Of a creature or human, looking backwards, over the shoulder.

**Respectant** Of two creatures or humans, looking at each other.

**Reversed** Of a weapon or tool, upside down, with the point downwards.

**Rompu (rompee)** Broken, of an *ordinary* or *sub-ordinary*.

**Rose en soleil** An Heraldic rose charged upon a *sun in splendour*. q.v.

**Roundle** A circle, of various colours, each having its own name.

**Rowel** The star-shaped object on the end of a spur.

**Royal** a full-grown red deer stag, synonymous with 'hart'.

**Rustre** A diamond-shaped figure with a hole in the middle. See *mascule* and *lozenge*.

### S

**Sable** Of the Heraldic *tinctures*, the colour black.

**Sagittarius** A *charge* representing *sagittary*, often with a drawn bow.

**Sagittary** A human monster, having the body of a lion joined to the torso of a man.

**Salamander** A mythical creature, lizard-like and supposed to be able to endure fire.

**Salient** Of a creature, leaping.

**Saltire** an ordinary, two crossed strips across the *shield*, diagonally, ('per saltire', the *field* divided in four parts, diagonally; 'in saltire' of charges set upon the shield in the plane of a saltire).

**Sanguine** Of the *tinctures* of Heraldry one of the *stains*, dark blood-red.

**Seal** A tool with an Heraldic device carved upon it, used to make an impression in wax, as a sign of authenticity; the wax impression itself.

**Seax** A curved, broad-bladed sword with a notch cut in the back.

**Saxon crown** An Heraldic *crown*.

**Seeded** Of a flower, denoting the colour of the centre of the flower; also of a pod, where the seeds show.

**Segreant** Of a griffin, as *rampant* is of a lion reared up to fight.

**Sejant** Of a beast, sitting upright facing *dexter*.

**Semy (semee)** Covered all over with small *charges*.

**Semee de lis** Covered all over with *fleurs de lis*.

**Seraphim** The first order of the angelic host.

**Shakefork** A Y-shaped *charge*, similar to a *pall* which does not reach to the edge of a *shield*.

**Shamrock** The three-leafed plant emblematic of Ireland; as a *charge*, shown *slipped*, with heart-shaped petals.

**Sheaf** A bundle of arrows, reeds, spears, synonymous with *garb*.

**Shield** The main defensive item of a man fighting on foot or horseback, used to ward off offensive blows. Nowadays the main item on which to display *armorial bearings*.

**Sinister** Left, considered from the point of view of the person bearing the *shield*, thus standing behind it.

**Sinople** Of the *tinctures* of Heraldry, the colour green in French usage.

**Slipped** Of a plant or flower, with a stem.

**Soaring** Of a winged creature, facing the front and flying with both wings outstretched.

**Sphinx** A mythical beast, usually represented as having the head of a woman and the (winged) body of a lion.

**Spur rowel** A star-shaped spike placed on a spur, synonymous in Heraldry with a pierced *mollet*.

**Stains** Colours of the *tinctures* of Heraldry that are not primary colours.

**Stall plate** Some of the orders of knighthood have their own chapels, in which members of the order display their armorial banners, each over his own seat, or stall. Past and deceased occupiers of a stall, whose banners have been taken down, have a metal, enamelled plate of their Achievement affixed to the stall.

**Statant** Of a creature, simply standing, facing the *dexter*.

**Standard** A long flag with a partly-coloured fringe, now displaying the arms, *crest*, motto and *livery colours* of the bearer.

**Star** In Heraldry represented as a figure with six wavy arms, called an *Estoil*; with five points it is called a *mollet*.

**Sub-ordinary** Any one of a group of the smaller, less frequently used, geometric shapes found as *charges*.

**Sunburst** A cloud with the sun's rays *issuant*.

**Sun in Splendour** The sun, issuing rays.

**Supporter** Any creature holding up a shield or helm, most commonly in pairs.

### T

**Tabard** A loose smock, without sleeves, on which *armorial bearings* are sometimes *emblazoned*

**Talbot** A large huntng dog with drooping ears, the model for representations of a hunting dog in Heraldry.

**Target** A *shield*, so named because it was at the shield that knights aimed their assaults during a *tournament*; usually of a small ceremonial sort, carried at a funeral; often abbreviated to 'targ'.

**Tau** A cross in the shape of a 'T', from that letter in the Greek Alphabet; known as a St. Anthony's Cross.

**Tenné (tenny)** Of the *tinctures* of Heraldry, one of the *stains*, tawny orange.

**Tiara** Usually refers, in Heraldry, to the papal headpiece of three *crowns*.

**Tincture** In Heraldry the term for all the colours employed.

**Tilting spear** Special spear used in *tournaments*.

**Tomb effigy** A prone statue of the deceased placed upon his tomb.

**Torse** A twist of material covering the joint between *crest* and *helm*, synonymous with 'wreath'.

**Torteau** A red roundle representing a cake of bread.

**Tressure** A narrow band placed on a *shield*, following its shape, but not touching the edge; usually found as a double tressure of two such bands; the two bands of a double tressure being a little wider than the one band of an *orle*.

**Transfixed** Pierced by a weapon.

**Trick** A shorthand way of nothing down a *blazon*.

**Tricorporate** Of a creature, having one head and three bodies.

**Triple-towered** A castle or tower with three smaller towers on top.

**Trippant (tripping)** Of deer, trotting or walking across the *shield* to the *dexter*, with one paw raised.

**Tufted** Of creatures, having tufts of hair on their knees, elbows, flanks, shoulders or chin.

**Tudor rose** An Heraldic rose, composed of a white rose charged upon a red rose, reversed, if placed upon a red field; occasionally found *quartered* and *counter-charged*, plain quartered or parted per *pale*.

**Tyger** An Heraldic creature, bearing little resemblance to a real tiger.

### U

**Undy** Of a *line of partition*, wavy.

**Unguled** Of the hoofs of a creature, in a separate specified colour.

**Unicorn** Fabulous horse monster with horn.

**Urchin** A hedgehog.

**Urdy** Of a *line of partition*, pointing, having points.

**Uriant** Of a fish, swimming down to the bottom of the *shield*.

**Umbrellino** See *pavilion*.

### V

**Vair** Of the *tinctures* in Heraldry, one of the furs, (blue and white).

**Vairy** Of a *field* of the *vair* type, but of specified *tincture*.

**Vallary crown** An Heraldic *crown*; (from the Roman tradition of bestowing a crown on the first to mount an enemy's rampart).

**Vambraced** Of an arm, protected by armour.

**Vert** Of the *tinctures* of Heraldry, one of the *colours*, green.

**Vested** See *habited*.

**Visor** The opening front of a helmet.

**Voided** Of a *charge*, appearing in outline only.

**Volant** Of a bird, flying across the *shield* with wings expanded.

**Vulned** Wounded and bleeding.

### W

**Wattled** Of a cock or other fowl, with skin hanging from the chin.

**Wavy** Of *lines of partition*.

**Woodwose (woodhouse)** A wild man of the woods, used as a *charge* and sometimes as a *supporter*.

**Wreath** See *torse*.

**Wreathy** Of a *subordinary*, depicted as if made like a wreath, with twists of cloth of various colours.

**Wyvern (wivern)** A mythical beast, being a winged dragon with two eagle-like feet and a barbed, serpentine tail.

### Y

**Yale** An Heraldic beast with horns and tusks.

# Index

**A**

Achievement of Arms, 2, 6, 7, 35, 36, 40, 41, 42, 43, 48, 53, 64
Acorned (tree), 80
Addorsed, 74
Affronty, 59
Agincourt, battle of, 30
Alligator, 74
Allusive Arms, 94–95
Alphonso VIII of Castille, 17
Alphonso IX of Leon, 17
Angels, 76, 78
Animals, as heraldic symbols, 61, 63, 69
 parts of body, 60
Antelope, 69
Archangels, 76, 78
Argent, 32, 53, 54, 58
Argyll, Duke of, 41
Arm, cuffed, 76, 77
 vambraced, 77
 vested, 76, 77
Armed, 74
Arms, confirming, 30
 devising of, 31
 entitlement to, 106
 granting of, 30, 53, 57
Astley of Norfolk (arms), 80
Augmentation (of coat of arms), 96
Avon County, 64
Azure, 53, 54, 58

**B**

Badger, 63
Badges, 20, 48, 106, 165
Bahamas, 74
Banners, 49, 52, 105
Barley, 81
Barnardiston, Sir Thomas, 50
Bayeux Tapestry, 20
Beacon, 91, 93
Beaked (bird), 74
Bear, 61, 63
Beasts, heraldic terms for, 59
Beatitudes, 85
Beaver, 61
Beddingfield, Sir Edward, 76
Bee, 76
Belled (bird), 74
Bere Regis Church, Dorset, 50
Berghersh, Richard, 60
Berrington of Chester, 53, 54
Bicorporate, 59
Birds, as heraldic symbols, 70–74
 Heraldic terms for, 74
Bittern, 70, 71
Black Prince, The, 97
Blazon, 53, 57, 76
Boar, 61, 63
 badge, 65
Bodies, celestial, 88
Bohun (arms), 63
Bonicon (monster), 69
Bouget, 90, 92
Bridge, 88
Broom (planta genesta), 80
Brittany, Duke of, 53, 54
Brock (badger), 63
Bruget of Normandy, 53, 54
Buck, 63
Buildings, as heraldic symbols, 88
Bull, 63

**C**

Caboshed, 60
Canon, illuminated, 78
Canting arms, 56, 58, 94
Caps, Napoleonic, 39
Carlisle roll, 31
Castle, 88
Cathedrals and Churches
 Bere Regis, Dorset, 50
 Christchurch, Oxford, 50
 Lincoln Cathedral, 60, 63, 80
 Long Melford, Suffolk, 24
 Norwich Cathedral, 6, 63, 80
 Bishop Goldwell Chantry, 63
 St. George's Chapel, Windsor, 49
 Salisbury Cathedral, 6
 Westminster Abbey, 68, 88
 Henry VII Chapel, 50
 St John The Baptist Chapel, 75
Celestial beings, 76, 78
Celestial bodies, 88
Centaur (monster), 81
Chains, 41, 106
Chapeau, 39
Charges, 54, 56, 57, 58, 96
 blazon, 57, 58
 canting arms, 56, 58
 combinations, 57, 58
 coronet, 39, 40
 counter-changing, 56, 58
 gutte, 56
 hereditary, 96
 ordinaries, 54, 55, 56
 sub-ordinaries, 56
 other, 56, 90
 roundels, 56
Charles I of Spain, 18
Cherub, 76
Chief, 57
China, for heraldic decoration, 107
Chivalry, medieval, 22
 orders of, 41, 106
 emblems of, 106
Christchurch, Oxford, 78
Christianity, 82
Churches, *see* Cathedrals and Churches
Cinquefoil, 80, 81, 84
Circlet, 106
Civic authorities, coats of arms
 Avon County, 64
 Beccles, Borough of, 43
 Chelmsford Borough Council, 48
 Cynon Valley, Borough of, 64
 Hambledon District Council, 80
 Lowestoft, Borough of, 79
Clarion, 90, 92
Close, 60, 74
Clopton, Ann, 50
Clopton, Sir Thomas, 20, 24
Clopton, Sir William, 20, 24, 50
Cloth, heraldic decoration on, 107
Clothing, 89
Clouds, 86
Coats of arms, 29, 30, 31, 32, 34, 41, 53, 54
 Royal Arms of England, 39, 78, 97
Cock, 70
Cockatrice (basilisk), 69
Columbine, 87
Colours, heraldic (tinctures), 32, 34
 argent, 32, 53, 54
 azure, 53, 54, 55, 58
 chart of, 34
 diapering, 32, 33, 35
 ermine, 32, 34
 ermines, 32, 34
 erminois, 32, 34
 pean, 32, 34
 for furs, 32
 for metal, 32
 gules, 58
 or, 32
 potent, 34
 rules, for use of, 34
 stains, 32
 vair, 32, 34
Combinations (charges), 56, 58
Commonwealth, 9, 10
Compartment, 48
Cooks, Worshipful Company of, 85
Cormorants, 70
Coronal (Cronal), 91, 93
Coronets, of rank, 40
Couchant (lion), 59, 61

Couped, 60
Counter-changing, 56, 58
Counter passant (lion), 61
Cowed, 62
Crest, 39, 40, 74
Crined, 59
Crocodiles, 76
Cromwell, Oliver, 10
Cross, heraldic, 41, 68, 88
 types of, 97
Crowned (bird), 74
Crowns, heraldic, 89
Crows, 72
Crozier, 104
Crusader, knights, orders of, 23, 83
Cushion, 91, 92

**D**

Daisy, 87
D'Arcy, Elizabeth, 19
D'Arcy, Thomas Lord, 6, 19
De Havilland and Howell (moulding), 80
De Hoeshpied, Baron, 96
De Mowbray, John, 23
De Walters (family), 96
Deer, 63
Demi, 59
Demi figure, 76
Denston, Anne, 24
Dexter (right), 31, 99
Diapering, 32, 34, 35
Differencing Arms Scottish System, 102, 103
Dimidiation, 96
Disarmed, 59
Displayed (bird), 60, 74
Divisions of field, 54
Dolphin, 74
Domestic items, 89
 hanger, 89
 clarion, 89
 flean, 89
 mill-rind, 89
Dormant (lion), 61
Double-headed, 60, 74
Double-queued, 59, 74
Dove, 70, 71
Dragon, 64
 red, of Wales, 64
Drury (family), 36
Duchy of Normandy, 9

**E**

Eagle, 72, 73
Earl Marshal of England, 40, 41
Ecclesiastical symbols, 76, 104
Edward III of England, 9
Elevated (bird), 74
Elizabeth, Queen of England, 10, 28
Embowed (fish), 74
Enfield (monster), 69
Entitlement, to arms, 106
Episcopal heraldry, 104, 105
Eradicated (tree), 80
Ersed (body), 60
Ermine (colour), 32, 34, 53, 54, 63
Escallop (shell), 75, 76
Escutcheon, of pretence, 97, 98

**F**

Face, 60
Falcon, 72, 73
Farmworkers, Worshipful Company of, 46
Farr (shield), 86
Ferdinand III of Castile and Leon, 17
Fesse-point, 31
Fetlock, 48, 91, 93
Field, heraldic, 54
 chief, 31
 divisions of, 54
 fesse-point, 31

nombril, 31
 partition, lines of, 54, 55
 semy, 54
Fish, as heraldic symbols, 74, 75, 76
 heraldic terms for, 74
Fishmongers, Worshipful Company of, 46
Flags, 50, 52
Flamingo, 74
Fleam, 90, 92
Fleur de Lys, 87
Flowers, heraldic, 38, 80, 81, 82–87
Fox, 63
Fraise (also frase and fraize), 80
Frederick of Sicilly, 17
Frogs, 63
*Froziart's Chronicles*, 76
Fructed (tree), 80

**G**

Garb, 80, 81
Gardner-Thorpe, Sir Ronald, 40
Glass, as heraldic medium, 107
Goat, 61
Gorged, 74
Granada, 18
Grenade, 91, 92
Gray, Jane (designer), 74, 88
Grid iron, 91, 93
Griffin, 42, 44, 69
Guardant, 59, 61
Gutte, 56, 57

**H**

Hale, Anne, 33
Hand of Ulster, 77
Hands, 76
Harpy (monster), 66, 67, 69
Hatchments, 48, 49, 76
Haurient (fish), 74
Head, 76
Hedgehog, 63
Heiress, heraldic, 98, 99
Helmet, heraldic terms, 37, 39, 40
 armet, 37
 barred, 37
 open visor, 37
 pot, 37
 tilting, 37
Henry IV of England, 9
Henry VII Chapel, Westminster Abbey, 50
Henwood (family), 57
Heraldic decoration, media for, 107
 tyger (monster), 69
Heraldry, language of, 31
 misconceptions about, 7
 origins of, 7
Heralds, 22, 28, 29
 and tournaments, 30
 as staff officer, 28, 29, 30
 role of, today, 30, 31
 arms, confirming, 30
 devising, 31
 granting, 30
Hertford, Countess of, 13
Hills, 91, 92
Holly leaf, 86
Horned, 59
Horse, 63
Hospitaliers, (order), 23
Hound, 63
House of Lords, 39
Howard, John, Duke of Norfolk, 52
Howard, Katherine, Lady, 52
Howard, Thomas, Duke of Norfolk, 23
Human beings, heraldic terms, 73, 74, 76
Hunsden, Lord, 75

**I**

Iceberg, 91, 93
Impalement, 96

Insects, 76
Insignia, of office, 40
Inverted (bird), 74

**J**

James I of England (VI of Scotland), 9
Jessant de lis, 60
Jessed (bird), 40, 72
Jewellery, as heraldic medium, 107
Joanna the Mad, 18
John of Aragon, 18
John II, Duke of Brabant, 16

**K**

Knights, orders of, 23, 29–30, 83
  Bath, the, 50, 52
  British Empire, the, 40
  Garter, the, 49, 52
  religious, 106
  St John, 40
  St Lazarus, 23
  Templars, 23
  Teutonic, 23

**L**

Lamb, 63, 69
Langued, 59
Lapwings, 70
Laurel, 87
Leather, as heraldic medium, 107
Lets, 76
Lily, 80, 86
Limbs, 60
Lincoln Cathedral, 54, 60, 63
Lines of partition (field), 54, 55
Lion, heraldic terms for, 59, 60, 61
  Lioncells, 61, 63
Livery colours, 107
Lizard, 76
Logan, Hart, 76
Long Melford Church, Suffolk, 24
Long Melford Hall, 28
Lotus, 87
Louis II, Count of Flanders, 16
Lowestoft, Borough of, 29
Lure, 72, 73

**M**

Mandrake, 66, 67, 69
Manfred of Sicily, 17
Manteau, 48
Mantelling (lambrequin), 40
Manvers, Baron, 41
Maple leaf, 80
Marden, F.G. (etcher), 64
Margaret, Heiress of Burgundy, 16
Marshalling arms, 96, 98
  dimidiation, 97
  escutcheon of pretence, 96, 97
  impalement, 96, 106
  quartering, 96, 97
  two shields together, 52
Martlet, 70, 71
Mary I of England, 14
Maunch, 90, 92
Maximillian, Archduke of Austria, 16
Medals, 41
Media, for heraldic decoration, 107
Melusin (monster), 66, 69
Membered (bird), 74
Mermaid, 69
Merman, 66, 67, 69
Military colours, 48
  roll, 24

Mill rind, 90, 92
Mitre, 104
Monpesson, Sir Richard, 6
Monsters, as heraldic symbols
  animals (winged), 64
  sea, 64
  mythological, 64
  human beings, composed of, 66, 67, 69
  more than one animal,
    composed of, 69
Moon, 88
Moorcock, 70, 73
More (augmentation), 96
Motto, 48

**N**

Naiant (fish), 74
Nails, Passion, 91, 93
Neville, Anne (wife of King Richard III), 65
Normandy, Duke of (William the Conqueror), 25
Norwich Cathedral, 6, 63, 80
  Bishop Goldwell Chantry, 63
Nombril, 31
Nowed, 59, 76

**O**

Oak leaves, 80, 81, 87
Octofoil, 85
Oliver, Stefan (engraver), 48, 76
Opinicus (monster), 69
Ordinaries, 54, 55, 56
Ounce (monster), 69
Our Lady, 85, 86
Owl, 70, 71

**P**

Pallium, 104
Palm, 87
Panther, 69
Papal heraldry, 104, 105
  cross keys of St Peter, 104
  tiara, 104
Paper, as heraldic medium, 107
Partition, lines, of, 54, 55
Passant (lion), 61
Peacock, 70, 71
Pelican, 70
Pennons, 52
Peter III of Aragon, 17
Philip I, Duke of Burgundy, 16, 18
Philip I of Spain and Sicily, 18
Philip II of Spain, 14
Philip the Bold, 16
Phoenix, 64
Plants, as heraldic symbols, 80, 81
Pomegranate, 91, 92
Porcupine crest, 68
Portcullis, 88
Pot, cooking, 91, 93
Prince of Wales badge, 74
Purse, 91

**Q**

Quatrefoil, 80, 81, 84
Quartering, 37, 52, 96, 97
Queue, 59
  fourchy (fourchee), 59, 60

**R**

Rabbit, 63
Rainbow, 88

Ram, 63
Ram, battering, 91, 95
Rampant, 60, 61, 63
Rank, coronets, of, 40
Regardant, 59
Religious orders, of chivalry, 106
Reptiles, as heraldic symbols, 76
  heraldic terms for, 76
Respectant, two lions, 61
Richard III, King of England, 65
Rising (bird), 60, 74
Rolls, of arms, 28, 30
  Carlisle, 31
  Rous, 65
Rook, chess, 90, 92
Rosary, 104
Rose, 80
  Heraldic, 85
  Tudor, of England, 80
Roundels, 56
Royal Arms of England, 78, 91, 93, 97
  chairback tapestry, 39

**S**

Sagittary (monster), 66, 67, 69
St George, 26, 76
St George's Chapel, Windsor, 49, 52
St John, Nicholas, 48
St John the Baptist Chapel,
  Westminster Abbey, 75
St Lazarus (order), 23
St Margaret, 79
Salamander, 64
Salient (lion), 61
Salisbury Cathedral, 6
Savage, Thomas Viscount, 6, 19
Scythe, 90
Sejant (lion), 61
Seraphin, 76
Shark, 74
Shield, types of, 31, 35, 53, 80
  Black Prince and brothers, 97
  ceremonial (Florentine), 35
  Farr (Lincoln Cathedral), 80
  describing of, 57
    blazon, 57
    trick, the, 57
  horse head, 36
  long, 35, 36
  lozenge, 365, 36, 37
  ornamental cartouches, 35
  oval, 35, 36, 37
  quartering of, 37, 52, 96, 97,
  short, 35, 36
  square, 35, 36
  two-coloured, 53, 54
  two together (arms), 52
  Weller, 34
Ships, as heraldic symbols, 89
Sinister (left), 31, 59, 99
Smith (families), 55
Snakes, 76
Soaring (bird), 60, 74
Solomon Islands, 74
Sphinx, 69
Spider, 76
Spur, 91, 93
Squirrel, 63
Staff, 104
Stafford, Lord Hugh, 26, 27
Stag, 63
Stained glass, 36
  window, 74, 88
Standards, 50
Stars, 88

Statant (lion), 61
Stork, 70, 71
Sub-ordinaries (charges), 56, 58
Sun, 48, 88
Sunflower, 87
Supporters (heraldic), 41, 42, 45, 48
Sussex, Countess of, 68
Swan, 70, 71
Sword fish, 74

**T**

Talbot, Elizabeth, 51
Talbot, John, Earl of Shrewsbury, 23
Templars (order), 23
Teutonic (order), 23
Thistle, 80, 81
Thunderbolt, 88
Tiger, 63
Tilney, Elizabeth, 23
Tilney, Sir Francis, 23
Tizard, Sir Peter, 88
Torse (wreath), 39
Tournaments, 22, 24, 30, 31
Tower, 88
Trees, as heraldic symbols, 80
Trefoil leaf, 80, 81, 84
Tricorporate, 59
Triton (monster), 66, 67, 69
Turberville (family), 50
Tufted, 59

**U**

Umbalino (ecclasiastical), 104
Unguled, 59
Unicorn, 64
United States of America, arms of, 79
Uriant (fish), 74

**V**

Vair (fur), 32, 34
Vellum, as heraldic medium, 107
Victoria I of England, 11
Volant (bird), 74
Vulned, 59
Vulning (bird), 74

**W**

Weapons, 89
Weller (shield), 80
Westminster Abbey, 13, 52, 68, 80
Westminster, Duke of, 88
Wheatears, 80, 81
Whelk shell, 75, 76
William III, Prince of Orange, 9
Windmill sails, 88
Winter, S & J (stone carving), 48, 88
Wolf, 63
Wood, as heraldic medium, 107
Wood (family), 74
Woodwose, 74, 76
Woolsack, 90, 92
Worshipful Company of Fishmongers, 69
Worshipful Company of Launderers, 74
Worshipful Company of Vintners, 79
Wyvern (monster), 64

**Y**

Yale (monster), 69

## Picture Credits

The British Library: pp 24 top, 28, 29.
Clive Hicks: pp 7, 20 top left, 21, 24
bottom, 48 top, 77 right, 60, 62, 80, 81
right, 51, 97, bottom.

Cognizance Heraldic Artwork Agency:
pp 21 top right, 29 top, 48 centre and
below, 57, 64, 74, 79, 76, 81 top left, 88
right, 89.

E T Archive: pp 2, 20, 30, 31, 33, 35, 36, 38,
42, 52, 54, 78, 65.
A F Kersting: pp 12, 13, 68, 75, 88 left, 49,
50, 51 top.

Wooden carving, illustrated on page 74,
by Derek Riley.
Moulded shields, illustrated on pages 64
and 81, by de Havilland and Howell.

## Acknowledgements

The author wishes to thank Marie Neal for her untiring and patient help in preparing this book, and the Cognizance Heraldic Artwork Agency for permission to reproduce photographs of the work of contemporary heraldic craftsmen. Thanks are also due to all those who have offered help and criticism, and to Lorraine Greenoak who precipitated the whole project.